HARLEY-DAVIDSON
KNUCKLEHEADS

Greg Field

Motorbooks International
Publishers & Wholesalers

The photographs from the Harley-Davidson Archives that appear in Greg Field's *Harley-Davidson Knuckleheads* are part of a large, important collection. Formerly housed at the Pohlman Photography Studios, the photos were taken under contract with The Motor Company or by virtue of personal relationships between the Pohlmans and the Davidsons and the Harleys. The collection from which the historical photos in this book were selected is an international treasure for all motorcycle enthusiasts.

The collection now resides in the Harley-Davidson Archives where it is being preserved and catalogued.

The Knucklehead era is one of the essential periods of Harley history, deserving continued exploration and analysis. Greg Field's book is a valuable resource, and the Harley-Davidson Archives is pleased to contribute historical photographs to enhance Mr. Field's text.

Dr. Martin Jack Rosenblum
Historian
Harley-Davidson Motor Company

First published in 1997 by Motorbooks International Publishers & Wholesalers, 729 Prospect Avenue, PO Box 1, Osceola, WI 54020-0001 USA

© Greg Field, 1997

Motorbooks International books are also available at discounts in bulk quantity for industrial or sales-promotional use. For details write to Special Sales Manager at the Publisher's address

Library of Congress Cataloging-in-Publication Data
Field, Greg.
Harley-Davidson Knuckleheads.
p. cm. — (Motorbooks color history)
Includes index.
ISBN 0-7603-0159-X (alk. paper)
1. Harley-Davidson motorcycle—Motors—History. I. Title.
II. Series: Motorbooks International motorcycle color history.
TL448.H3F53   1997
629.25—dc21   97-8166

On the front cover: Eldon Brown is the proud owner/restorer of this beautiful 1939 EL. The solid wheels are period-correct accessories, made by Wolfe Wheel Company of Akron, Ohio, that have been on the bike since it was new.

On the frontispiece: The instrument panel, shifter gate, and Brooke Stevens-designed tank emblem were all new for 1947. They would be carried over to the Panhead beginning in 1948.

On the title page: First- and second-year Knuckleheads. Both bikes belong to owner/restorer Carman Brown.

On the back cover: Top: Dave Banks' 1936 EL and Ron Lacey's 1939 pose in front of Banks home. Bottom: Harley-Davidson speed maven Joe Petrali aboard the specially built Knucklehead he rode to a new AMA straightaway record of 136.183 miles per hour on the sands of Daytona Beach. *Copyright Harley-Davidson Michigan, Inc.*

Edited by Lindsay Brooke
Designed by Katie Finney
Printed in Hong Kong through World Print, Ltd.

CONTENTS

Acknowledgments

I never could have imagined what a monumental project this book turned out to be. Without the help and encouragement of dozens of individuals, it would still be just a bunch of disorganized rantings on my computer's hard drive, so I offer my thanks to the following:

First, to the foremost scholars of the 1936 Knucklehead, who were so helpful in my Quixotic quest to tabulate the zillion-and-one changes made to the Knucklehead that first year. Because of the effort of these men, Chapter 1 of the Knucklehead saga is much more complete: Jerry Hatfield, Chris Haynes, Casey Hoekstra, Doug Leikala, and Gerry Lyons.

For letting me photograph their fine Knuckleheads: Dave Banks, Carman Brown, Eldon Brown, Rob Carlson, and Gary Strom of Kokesh Motorcycles (Spring Lake Park, Minnesota), Jeff Coffman of Jeff's American Classics (Dundee, Oregon), Jim "Aard" Conklin, Dave DeMartini of Northwest Custom Cycle (Snoqualmie, Washington), Valentino "Vick" Domowicz, Elmer Ehnes, Larry Engesether, Farmer Fred, Mike Golembiewski, Ron Lacey, Dave Monahan, Adolph Ogar, and Wayne Pierce, Sr. and Wayne Pierce, Jr., of Pierce's Harley-Davidson in DeKalb, Illinois.

For sharing their knowledge, time, photographs, or for helping me to find motorcycles to photograph: Rick Connor, Peter Eagan, George "Geo" Edwards of St. Paul Harley-Davidson (St. Paul, Minnesota), Brian Holden of the Deeley Motorcycle Museum (Vancouver, British Columbia), Rick "Chintzy" Krajewski of Competition Cycle (Milwaukee, Wisconsin), Dave Minerva, Gary Nelson, Bruce Palmer, Jerry Renner, and Steve Schlessinger at Jerry's House of Harley (Milwaukee, Wisconsin), Scott Rowinski, Carmen Tom of Downtown Harley-Davidson (Seattle, Washington), and Herbert Wagner.

For helping me with research material and photographs, the Harley-Davidson Motor Company, and in particular, Dr. Martin Jack Rosenblum and Susan Fariss in the archives and Ray Schlee in the restoration shop. Black-and-white photographs are courtesy of the Harley-Davidson Motor Company archives. All rights reserved.

For long-term encouragement and support to my parents, Laurie and Larry, my brothers and sisters, Scot, Shawn, Dawn, and Heather, and my good friends Owen Herman, Tim Lien, Tom Samuelsen, John Scharf, and Joe Sova.

For putting me up and putting up with me while in Milwaukee: Annie and Tobie Golembiewski; Ray, Carol, Becky, Katie, Tracy, Vicky, and Nicole Karshna; Ed and Jean Kwiecinski; and Jeff and Jackie Ciardo.

For tangible and intangible support to Keith, Jerry, Peter, Dustin, and Steve at the fabulous, motorcycle-friendly Buckaroo in Seattle.

For tolerating my "fluid" deadlines, editor Zack Miller and the rest of the staff of Motorbooks International.

Finally, to Jeni, who put up with so much obsessive behavior and gave up so much so that I had time to finish this manuscript.

If I have forgotten anyone, I hope they will forgive the oversight.

Knuckleheads at play. Three or four Knuckles are usually ridden in each show by the famous Seattle Cossacks precision motorcycle drill team. Yes, they really can hold the pyramid through a turn to reverse direction within the width of a street, and yes, that Cossack at the very back is doing a handstand between the bikes.

CHAPTER ONE

1936

The First Knucklehead

H istory is not often made in a ballroom, but it was on November 25, 1935. On that day, at the annual dealers' convention—after years of rumors and sporadic sightings—the assembled throng of Harley-Davidson dealers was treated to a vision of their future, the company's future. When the curtains parted, there stood parked upon the stage of the Green Room in Milwaukee's Shroeder Hotel a new motorcycle so different, so right, so inspired that the "eager, anxious crowd [leapt] to its feet and burst into prolonged cheers," according to the account in the January 1936 issue of *The Enthusiast.* Standing beside the new "61 OHV," chief engineer William S. Harley and "Hap" Jameson soaked up the adulation for their new baby. It was the day the legend began.

Dave Banks' EL, the 374th built, has the round tin covers on the rocker-shaft ends. Sometime during the production run, these covers were replaced by large chrome-plated hex nuts. Also during the production run, an air fitting was added to the front rocker housing that allowed the rider to clear clogged oil return lines from the valve-spring covers by applying air pressure to the nipple. Banks' bike was never retrofitted with the nipple. His bike also has the "notched" gear case cover used on early machines. Note the hole in the surface of the gear case, just aft of the brake pedal. Shown in the hole is one of the two rivets used to attach the breather baffle to the inside of the case. The holes for these rivets were sometimes leaded over. Years of engine vibration sometimes makes the lead plugs pop out, as these have.

After impatiently enduring the presentation of the whole 1936 line-up, the dealers rushed the stage to get a closer look at the new flagship of the line, Harley's new "little Big Twin." The machine before them was a masterpiece from any angle, a bold fusion of art deco and streamlining that looked both fast and mannered. More important, it looked like a *motorcycle,* as if it had been created that way, rather than—having slowly evolved from the first motorized bicycles that H-D had built. In fact, the only throwback to that heritage seemed to be the bicycle pedal on the kickstarter. The more the dealers looked, the more they appreciated it.

Symmetry defined the new machine. Twin gas tanks straddled the frame's backbone tube, each with its own chrome-plated filler cap and petcock. Bridging the gap between the tanks was the new instrument panel with a large, integral, 100-mile-per-hour speedometer (placed front and center, right where it would be easiest to read), an ammeter, an oil-pressure indicator, and the ignition switch. Twin downtubes swept down and back from the steering head to the rear axle clips. The sweeping V of the cylinders, highlighted on the right side by the gleaming pushrod covers, framed the dramatically slash-cut chrome-plated air-intake horn. And those cylinders were topped by polished aluminum rocker housings, each with two round, chrome-plated covers over the ends of the rocker shafts. It was everything the rumors said—and everything the dealers had hoped it would be. As far as the dealers were concerned, this was the Eighth Day, and creation was complete.

Enthusiasm for the new model spilled over to the banquet that evening, and after soaking up copious amounts of the famous Milwaukee "suds," some of the dealers got a little out of

An early-1936 61 owned and restored by Carman Brown of British Columbia. The 1936 61 introduced the most enduring aesthetics of any motorcycle. From end to end, it was a masterpiece, and elements of its style are evident on all the Harley-Davidson Big Twins that followed. This was no beefed-up motorized bicycle. This, at last, was a motorcycle. The only throwback to its older siblings was the bicycle-style kickstarter pedal.

control. During the turkey dinner, "two-gun 'Cactus Bill' Kennedy, a tough hombre from Phoenix, Arizona, [got] so excited . . . he [drew] a bead on the crystal chandelier, let out a blood-curdling yip-eee . . . and emptie[d] his six-gun . . . some of the more sedate dealers pass[ed] out . . . and the turkey on Bill's plate actually turn[ed] pale," according to *The Enthusiast*.

In the following days, the dealers toured the factory and attended sales seminars. History has not recorded whether H-D gave their dealers any further information on when the new model would be ready, but a curious thing happened after the curtain was drawn closed on the Green Room's stage: The most exciting new American motorcycle in over a decade disappeared as completely as if it had never been there at all. When Harley's 1936 models were announced to the public in the January 1936 issue of *The Enthusiast*, the new model—a machine that was truly innovative enough to warrant a good bit of hype—was not shown or mentioned at all. In fact, the only clue to its existence was in a small photograph of the assembled dealers at the November convention. Way in the background of the photo, appearing so small that you'd have to know it was there to make it out, was the new

machine. But the caption for the photo made no mention of it, nor did the magazine's coverage of the convention. And so it would go, far into the machine's first year of production.

To the Harley-Davidson Motor Company, the enthusiasm of its dealers was welcome, but it also presented a quandary. After more than four years of spending heavily to develop the OHV, Harley was eager to begin recouping its costs, but knew well what would happen if the new model was released before it was ready. Still smarting from the disastrous introduction of its last new Big Twin, the company decided on a more cautious approach this time.

Roots of the 61

The company's past had been built on the foundation of its early intake-over-exhaust, or F-head, engines that gave it such success from 1903 to 1929. The company's present was being built on the newer side-valve, or flathead, engines that were introduced in 1929 (45-ci Series D) and 1930 (74-ci Series V), but these models proved to be disappointing in many ways. Initially, both proved to be trouble-prone, especially the V series, which had so many problems that the production line was shut down to fix them after a flood of dealer complaints gave H-D no other choice. To its credit, the company stood by its product, redesigning many parts to fix the problems on the production line and sending free kits to fix those bikes already on the streets. But the initial blunder had eroded confidence among the company's dealers and customers. They had to wonder: was it an honest mistake, or was Harley-Davidson inept and past its prime?

By 1931, most of the inadequacies of the first V-series machines had been fixed. Still, Harley's side-valve models were somewhat disappointing because they were not that much better than the old F-heads they replaced. Worse yet, they suffered in performance compared to the equivalent Indian models. In short, the Harley side-valves were decent motorcycles, but they weren't exciting motorcycles, certainly not exciting enough to win new customers—especially when times were so hard for so many. The company needed something radically new on which to build its future.

The Great Depression Begins

Motorcycle sales had been up and down for many years, but the trend was definitely down in 1931. In contrast, the trend had been up during the boom years of 1927–1929 when the side-valves were introduced. In 1929, H-D sold 23,989 machines, the largest number sold since 1918, when sales of military bikes inflated annual sales to 26,708. Then came "Black Thursday," October 24, 1929, when the stock market collapse began. On October 29, "Black Tuesday," the real crash came. Stock prices went into a death spin. In one week, $16 billion evaporated.

Reverberations from the crash spread slowly across America in 1930. In the early part of the year, the stock market began to recover. And those with wealth remained optimistic. Henry Ford, who had sold his one-millionth Model A the year before, opined that, "These really are good times but

This photo shows what may be the actual machine that met with such enthusiasm at the dealers' meeting at the Schroeder Hotel in Milwaukee, Wisconsin, on November 25, 1935—serial number 35E1002. This machine and the others like it (there were at least three, and there were thought to be as many as a dozen) are commonly referred to as the "pre-production" 1936 61s. It is not known when they were built, but certainly before October 17, 1935, when this photo was processed. Because it wears a 1935 serial number, it may in fact be a demonstrator model built when the bike was still slated for a late-1935 introduction. The valve springs are visible behind the oil fittings on the rocker housings, denoting the absence of valve-spring covers on the preproduction machines. A photo of oil-drenched 35E1003 that follows graphically shows how necessary the valve-spring covers were. Note the stamping "Burgess Battery Co." on the side of the muffler. This name is not commonly seen on the sides of production mufflers, but was sometimes stamped on the underside of the muffler, in much smaller letters. Also note the round, chrome-plated covers over the ends of the rocker-arm shafts on the aluminum rocker housings. *Copyright Harley-Davidson Michigan, Inc.*

only a few know it." Men of more modest means really did know better, and they were not in a spending mood, especially for something as frivolous as a motorcycle. Then came the final nail in the economic coffin: Congress passed the Smoot-Hawley Act in June, which sharply raised tariffs. In retaliation, other countries raised theirs. Unemployment rose further, and H-D's export sales, which had been as much as 40 percent of the company's business during the 1920s, dropped off sharply. When the results were tallied at the end of the fiscal year, Harley-Davidson's overall sales for the year dropped by nearly 25 percent, to 18,036. The Great Depression had begun.

Bill Harley's "Sump Oiler"

Which brings us back to 1931, a desperate and historic year. As alluded to earlier, the trend was down in 1931. Way down. Sales fell to 10,407, slightly more than half the number sold the previous year and the lowest total since the 3,853 sold in 1912! Clearly, the company was in trouble. Salaries had been cut, and hours had been slashed for nonsalaried workers. But

despite the gloom, William S. Harley never gave up. Instead, in a flash of inspiration worthy of the great Thomas Edison, he proposed development of the motorcycle that would ultimately save the company—an OHV twin with a recirculating oil system, referred to as the "sump oiler." The board of directors gave its approval, and work began on what would ultimately be the 61 OHV. And here's where our story really begins.

If 1931 was a year of hardship—and it was—1932 was worse. The Dow dropped below 50. Over two million Americans wandered the country as vagrants. Unemployment rose to 24 percent overall, but reached 50 percent in some cities. Along with it, the suicide rate rose 30 percent.

Hard times grew worse in Milwaukee, too. Harley-Davidson workers were laid off, and the company's four founders imposed on themselves a 50 percent pay cut. Production fell to 7,218, a reduction of 30 percent compared to the previous year. But a new source of income was in the offing. The board of directors was approached by its Japanese importer and the Sankyo industrial firm with an offer to purchase a

Preproduction machine 35E1003 partially disassembled to show the new top end that made the 61 so exciting—and so troublesome. This preproduction machine was probably one of the unmarked road-test machines, as implied by the lack of tank decals. The cylinder heads lack provision for valve-spring covers, accounting for the oil-spattered appearance of the machine. The head on the right shows raised casting numbers on the bottom fin (casting numbers were usually recessed on production heads). The oil tank shows evidence that an earlier version of the oil tank had fittings farther out to the side. Note the welded-in plug on the side of the tank (there is another on the other side of the tank). Tanks with these plugs made it onto some production 1936 61s. The plug was leaded smooth before painting to hide the repair. Note the "notched" gear-case cover, a feature that also made it onto the early production machines. Note also the two pinstripes on the fenders. Finally, note the slash-cut, single-butted joint on the frame downtubes and the lack of sidecar lugs. This photo was processed on November 14, 1935, just over a week before the 61's debut at the dealers' convention. *Copyright Harley-Davidson Michigan, Inc.*

license to manufacture H-D motorcycles in Japan—an offer that was ultimately accepted. As bad as things got, however, work continued on the OHV.

Things really bottomed out in Milwaukee in 1933. Harley sales fell by almost half again, to just 3,703 machines. But things also began looking up. Prototype parts for the new 61 were cast and assembled into working engines. Bench tests were promising, so the board agreed to continue development and scheduled the OHV to be their lead model for 1935. The board also approved the sale of a manufacturing license to the Sankyo firm in Japan. Sankyo began setting up to produce the Harley-Davidson VL under the trade name Rikuo.

The Depression slowly began to ease its grip on the economy in 1934. The Dow rose only slightly, but the gross national product (GNP) rose 17 percent (versus shrinking by 4 percent in 1933). Harley sales nearly tripled for 1934, to 11,212

units—aided by the late introduction of 1935 models, which occurred in December, rather than in September. Unfortunately, development of the 61 OHV had fallen behind schedule, so when the 1935 models were announced, the 61 OHV was not among them. The first rideable machine had been assembled and tested in the spring and summer of 1934, but nagging problems with oil leaks prevented finalization of the design in time for 1935 production. The board of directors delayed introduction of the new model until 1936.

The United States' recovery accelerated somewhat in 1935. The Dow rose to a high of 144. The GNP grew 9 percent, and unemployment declined to near 20 percent.

In Milwaukee, Harley-Davidson's OHV was nearing completion in the summer of 1935. According to board of directors minutes unearthed by author Jerry Hatfield and presented in his book, *Inside Harley-Davidson*, there was even discussion of building 200 61s in the summer of 1935 but the sales department was opposed to the idea because it feared release of the 61 would adversely affect sales of the remaining 1935 side-valve Big Twins.

At the May meeting, the board discussed releasing the 61 in September 1935 or January 1936, even though continuing problems with chain and brake-lining wear caused some members of the board to suggest that the 61 project be stopped entirely. Company president Walter Davidson suggested that a different combination of sprockets might reduce chain wear. Davidson's suggestions apparently resulted in changing the transmission sprocket from 19 teeth to 22 teeth and the rear sprocket from 45 teeth to 51 teeth (based on data in the book *1930 to 1949 Models: Operation, Maintenance, and Specifications*, published by Harley-Davidson), which resulted in enough of an improvement that the board resolved that it would "probably go ahead with the job" at its June meeting. Although it is not recorded in the minutes, continuing difficulties with the 61 may have resulted in the decision to push back the new-model introduction into the winter for the second year in a row.

Oil Control

The big problem that remained to be solved was control of oil to and from the rocker arms and valves. On the prototype 61s, the valves, valve springs, and rocker arms were left uncovered. Many other OHV machines of the day also had uncovered mechanisms, but the rockers on those machines were typically lubricated by grease that was periodically resupplied through a grease fitting. Not so on the 61 engine; its signature feature, the OHV system, was lubricated by oil bled off from the engine's other great, new feature, its recirculating oil system. I say "bled off" because any lubricating oil supplied to lubricate the rockers, valves, and springs eventually ended up on the outside of the engine. And once the oil escaped the valve mechanism, the slipstream quickly carried it back to splatter all over rider and machine.

Approval for Production

As summer turned to fall, the solution to the oiling problem apparently proved elusive. Unfortunately, the new-model introduction date was fast approaching, and having already delayed the 61 OHV's introduction by a year, the company's managers were loathe to delay it any longer. At the October board meeting, the 61 was officially added to the line-up for 1936, and production was set for 1,600 units. No one knows whether approval came as a result of a long-sought solution to the oil-control problem or whether was made the decision with crossed fingers, trusting that luck and Bill Harley's design acumen would reveal a solution to the problem before full-scale production began. Evidence suggests the latter because photographs that were developed as late as December show no evidence of valve-spring enclosures on the 61.

Preproduction 61 OHVs

Consensus among many 1936 61 aficianados is that Harley-Davidson built a dozen or so preproduction machines for continued testing, for presentation at the convention and

Front and center on the skull-face instrument panel is a Stewart-Warner speedometer with a 100-mile-per-hour face, which was used only for 1936 on the 61. For 1937, the speedometer was calibrated up to 120 miles per hour because a well-tuned EL could come very close to outrunning the 100-mile-per-hour speedometer. The dice gearshift knob was included in the Deluxe Solo Group or was available for 60 cents at the time the bike was ordered.

for photography. No records exist to tell how many were built or when they were built, but we can conclude a few things from existing photographs: at least two 61s were built with 1935 serial numbers; at least one of these was extensively road-tested; and the road-test machine leaked a lot of oil because it still lacked covers for the rockers and valves.

The first conclusion is based on photos that show the motorcycles serial numbered 35E1002 and 35E1003. The second conclusion is supported by the engine-teardown photo of 35E1003, which shows the bike coated in grime and oil, and its kickstarter pedal shows wear from use and damage from a light spill or tip-over. The same photo supports the third conclusion, clearly showing that no valve-spring covers were used on these machines.

These photos also provide the only reliable time reference that is available to date the preproduction bikes. The photos of 35E1002 were processed October 17, 1935. The photos of the oil-soaked 35E1003 were processed on November 14, 1935, and were described as "motor close-ups for Joe Ryan." (Joe Ryan was H-D's service manager.) From this we can conclude that these preproduction machines had been completed no later than mid-October, more than a month before the 61's introduction at the convention.

The 61s serialed 35E1002 and 35E1003 are considered preproduction machines rather than experimental prototypes because their serial numbers are in the form of production serial numbers, rather than the form of experimental serial numbers (EX 3, for example). The serial numbers on these machines could also be taken as further proof that the 61 had been originally planned for the 1935 model line. The 61 OHV displayed at the November dealers' convention was likely one of these preproduction machines. Ultimately, these machines were probably scrapped.

Another British Columbian 1936 61, this one owned by Dave Banks. The Venetian Blue and Croydon Cream paint scheme shown was probably the most popular of its day, and it still is today, judging by the high percentage of machines that are restored to these colors.

Stealth Introduction

In the first dealer news bulletin following the dealers' convention—dated December 2, 1935—Harley-Davidson issued its first printed words about the 61 to make it clear to all that the new model was not yet ready and that it might not be for some time:

For several years rumors have been current all over the country about a new twin that Harley-Davidson was developing and would have on the market any day. The most incredulous and many times positively amusing fabrications have been spread about this model. True, our engineering staff has been working for a long time on a model of new and original design and their efforts have finally reached the stage where such a motorcycle, a 61 cubic inch overhead, was shown to dealers in attendance at the National Dealers' Convention. However, production on this model will necessarily be extremely limited and we are therefore in no position to make a public announcement at this time. . . . Under no circumstances should this model be ordered as a demonstrator!

But as we shall soon see, even as the company was admonishing its dealers not to order OHV demonstrators, the assembly line was being readied for their production. Moreover, the new model had already been listed in a specification sheet for standard and special equipment groups dated December 1, 1935.

Pilot Production

Clearly, the company remained uneasy about the 61 despite dealer enthusiasm. One of the things that made them uneasy was undoubtedly the lack of an effective means to return oil from the valve-gear to the engine. Despite their unease—according to Hatfield's *Inside Harley-Davidson*, based on the minutes of the December 16, 1935, board of directors meeting—company managers had earlier made the decision to press on, building "10 or 15" pilot production bikes by mid-December to "check the flow of parts through the various buildup levels." The famous photo of the four company founders with what was reputed to be the first production 61 OHV was developed on December 12, 1935, and shows the founders with one of these pilot production bikes. No documentation exists to prove when the top-end oil-control problem was solved—which it eventually was, through introduction of cup-type valve-spring covers with oil return lines—but it was after the build date of the pilot production 61 pictured with the company founders because that machine definitely does not have the valve-spring covers.

15

A view inside the gear case showing how the cams, breather valve, and ignition circuit breaker are timed and how engine power is routed to power the oil pump and generator. *Copyright Harley-Davidson Michigan, Inc.*

The disassembled clutch on 35E1003, showing the major parts: splined drum, splined hub, pressure-plate/drive-plate assembly with springs, fiber discs with splines on their outside diameter, and steel discs with splines on their inside diameter. On production 1936 clutches, a "humped" steel disc was fitted in place of one of the flat steel discs in an effort to reduce rattle when the clutch was disengaged. This style of clutch was used through 1940. This early-style inner primary cover lacks the oil drain fitted to later covers because the oil drain is in the outer cover on early machines. *Copyright Harley-Davidson Michigan, Inc.*

After assembly, the first pilot-production machines were then turned over to the engineering department for road-testing. Apparently, problems were experienced with the motors because, "Most of these first production 61 OHVs were returned to the motor assembly section for reworking," according to Hatfield. The early production-line problems were apparently resolved by the December 16 date of the board meeting because, continued Hatfield, "Most reworking was by this time sufficiently infrequent and minor to be accomplished on the assembly line."

Unfortunately, we don't know what happened to the "10 or 15" pilot production machines. It is possible, as other authors have speculated, that some were sent to favored dealers for independent road-testing. If so, these bikes may have been the source of the much-repeated stories of "laps full of oil" after even a short test ride, since the pilot production machines almost certainly did not have the valve-spring covers. We know that these bikes were built in calendar-year 1935, so the engine cases *should* have been stamped with line-bore numbers having a "35" prefix (35-1234). None of the 1936 61 specialists I have spoken to have ever seen cases so marked—which, of course, proves nothing, but hints that either the bikes were scrapped after testing, that they have all disappeared, or that they were marked with "36" line-bore numbers.

With the assembly-line procedures debugged, it would seem that H-D was potentially ready to begin full-scale production of the 61 OHV, but did it? Along with this question, many others come to mind. Did pilot production just gradually ramp up after the December 16, 1935, meeting to become regular production of demonstrator models for the dealers, or was production delayed while further changes were instituted to the 61 design or assembly-line procedures? If there was a delay, was it caused by the need to solve the rocker-oiling problem? Was the rocker-oiling problem even solved by the time production began? Unfortunately, documentation to conclusively answer these questions has yet to surface, but a few clues to the time line for production were found in the Harley-Davidson archives, which I'll get to in due course.

Given their lack of experience with production OHV systems and the truly wretched economy at the time, Harley-Davidson took a big gamble in introducing its new OHV Big Twin. The enthusiastic reception the motorcycle had received at the dealers' convention had to ease Harley-Davidson's fears somewhat, but only the sales year to come would really reveal whether American riders would pay extra for the new engine design—and whether the new engine was really ready for those who would.

Window to the World, 1936

The withering effects of the Great Depression and the Dust Bowl continued in 1936, but in the United States the New Deal was really starting to seem like a better deal. For the third straight year, unemployment was down, although at 16.9 percent it was still shockingly high by modern standards. And the Dow and GNP were both up for the second year in a row. In an overwhelming vote of confidence for his policies, President Roosevelt was reelected in an electoral landslide.

Around the world, the Fascists began to march. Francisco Franco led his army against the republic for control of Spain. Germany and Italy joined in to test their burgeoning military might and help out their ally. And Mussolini's Italian Army continued its march across Ethiopia, occupying all of that country before the year was out.

After claiming dictatorial power in 1933, rubbing out his competitors in 1934, and instituting a state program for breeding perfect Aryans in 1935, Hitler began to reclaim lands Germany lost in the Treaty of Versailles.

Hitler also sought conquest in the world of sports, turning the 1936 Olympics, held in Berlin, into a shameless showpiece for Aryan superiority. Despite the best efforts of the "superior" elite of Aryan manhood, the "inferior" African-American athletes on the U.S. team dominated the prestigious track-and-field events.

Dale Carnegie's *How to Win Friends and Influence People* became a best-seller by simply telling people how to succeed by getting along with others. Apparently Hitler did not buy a copy.

If any two groups needed Carnegie's book, it was the United Auto Workers and the automotive industry management. Strained relations between them broke down, resulting in crippling strikes at a Fisher Body plant, at Midland Steel, and at Kelsey-Hayes Wheel. Fortunately, Harley-Davidson had an adequate supply of rims before the Kelsey-Hayes strike.

Production Begins

One of the great mysteries of the enigma that is the 1936 Knucklehead is when production really began. Some say it began in December 1935. Others maintain that it wasn't until March or April. The principals who had firsthand knowledge are all dead, and definitive documentation from within the Harley-Davidson archives has yet to surface. If it is there, I couldn't find it on two separate research visits, so I don't have the definitive answer—but I have uncovered some interesting facts that shed some light on the timeline.

Remember that admonition in the December 2, 1935, dealer news bulletin that "Under no circumstances should this model be ordered as a demonstrator!"? Well, just over one month later, the factory had obviously taken orders for the demonstrators and was well on its way to filling those orders. The January 27, 1936, dealer news bulletin trumpeted the headline "61 Overhead Twin Demonstrators Now Being Shipped!" The article beneath the headline went on to say, "Demonstrator orders for the new 61 Overhead Valve Twin are moving out at a healthy rate and production in the factory is gradually picking up." Of course, "healthy rate" and "picking up" are not very illuminating, but they do indicate that 61s were definitely rolling off the production line by the deadline date for the bulletin.

And the bikes shipped on or near that deadline date were obviously not the first machines out the door because that same news bulletin went on to say, "Reports from dealers who have already received their 61 demonstrators indicate that the new model is proving a real sensation and is exceeding all expectations."

Even more revealing is an actual report from a dealer, Kemper Motorcycle Company in Chicago, Illinois, because it reveals that the factory was by this time (late January) allowing the dealers to sell, or at least take orders for, the new 61s: "Just got in the 61 floor sample this A.M. Everybody likes it. Sold one today and expect two more to trade."

We also know that at least one 61 OHV had been shipped as far west as Portland, Oregon, on or before February 2, 1936, because a rider named "Butch" Quirk used a sidecar-equipped 61 to win the 350-mile endurance run sponsored by the Rose City Motorcycle Club, as reported in the March issue of *The Enthusiast.* Surely, this bike was shipped from Milwaukee no later than the last week of January.

The February 10, 1936, bulletin showed that favorable reports had been returned to the factory from as far away as California and Texas. The firm of Graves & Chubbuck in Pasadena wrote: "There never has been a motorcycle put out that has set the boys to talking so much as the 61. The news of its arrival was broadcast by the boys from the treetops, and five hours after its setup there was 120 miles on the speedometer." From Fort Worth came the report that "this is the first machine that no rider or prospect could find fault with, as they have nothing but praise for it." These bikes must also have left Milwaukee no later than the end of January.

The next issue of the news bulletin lends some credence to the notion that the demonstrators were really just the first production configuration machines and implies that regular series production began some time around mid-February. A headline in the February 24 bulletin announced, "We Are Surging Right Along on the 61!" The article beneath said, "Demonstrator orders for the 61 have all been taken care of and we are now making satisfactory deliveries on dealers' subsequent orders."

Apparently, the factory was not yet mobbed with orders by the deadline for the February 24 issue, so at long last the factory began prodding their dealers to get out and sell the 61 because the much-anticipated new model was at last available. The article continued: "We can't guarantee this state of affairs will continue indefinitely, but right now there is no very long delay in getting out orders. If some of your good customers have been under the impression that they couldn't get their 61's for a long time, better tip them off that if they place their order right away, they can get their machine before long. A little later when the remarkable qualities of the new model are better appreciated and when the real riding season opens, there may be considerable delay in getting deliveries."

About the time the dealer bulletin exhorted the dealers to push the 61 OHV, the new bike received its first official mention in the national press when it was shown in an ad in the March 1936 issue of *The Motorcyclist.* Even in this first ad, however, the 61 was given no special mention, let alone hype. Earlier, in January, the company had not even shown or mentioned the 61 in the new-model introduction issue of *The*

Enthusiast. In fact Harley-Davidson would make no official mention of the 61 in their own magazine until June 1936.

So where does this leave us? We still can't say for sure exactly when series production began, but it probably started slowly in early January and began ramping up from there until late February, when the factory was able to crank out new bikes at least as fast as the orders came in. By that time, the factory was confident enough about the 61 that it was asking its dealers to actually sell it, but it was still hesitant to give it the usual sales hype. The first hint of sales hype came in the June issue of *The Enthusiast*, which featured a back-cover ad for the 61.

Another big mystery is the exact configuration of the demonstrators. Were they regular production machines? Did they have the valve-spring covers? The glowing reports would seem to indicate that they did, for how could a rider not fault a motorcycle that slung as much oil as the 61s without valve enclosures are reputed to have?

Then comes the mystery of configuration of the first production models—indeed, the configuration of all the 1936 61s. During the production year, many parts of the 1936 61 were changed in subtle and not-so-subtle ways to improve the function of the machine and to fix problems that became apparent as the bikes were used in competition and on the street. A complete list of all the changes for 1936, with even the most cursory description of the parts and what was changed, could easily fill a book this size. Since the scope of this book is much broader, covering all the Knuckleheads from 1936 through 1947, the discussion presented here is incomplete, by necessity, and will concentrate on the changes that are obvious or important in describing later model Knuckleheads.

1936 Models and Prices

Although the new OHV model did not appear in the January issue of *The Enthusiast*, which introduced the rest of the 1936 line, order blanks featuring the model had been quietly sent to dealers. The order blanks listed the OHV Big Twin in three versions: the high-compression 36EL Special Sport Solo, the medium-compression 36E Solo, and the medium compression 36ES twin with sidecar gearing. All were listed at a retail price of $380, but this was without such essential equipment as a jiffy stand or a steering damper. These items were available at additional cost or as part of the option groups. Interestingly, a Model 36EM "Twin Motor For Midget Car Racing" is listed in the back of *The Legend Begins*, published by H-D.

Wheelbase for all models was 59.5 inches and weight was 515 pounds. The main differences between the models was in compression ratio and gearing. The EL engine was fitted with high-compression pistons for a compression ratio of 6.5:1 and a power output of 40 horsepower at 3,800 rpm, according to Harley-Davidson specifications. The E and ES engines were fitted with medium-compression pistons for a compression ratio of 5.66:1 and a power output of 37 horsepower at 3,800 rpm. Interestingly, the compression ratios for the E and ES are listed as being the same, even though the

Here's 35E1003 again, this time with its rear wheel removed. The wheel hub is fastened to the brake drum by lug bolts. Each lug has a safety-wire hole. Lugs with safety-wire holes were fitted for at least part of the 1936 production run. The 7 1/4-inch rear brake shown was used on the 1936 61 only. The type of rear mount for the rear chain guard shown did not make it into production. It did not even make it onto one of the other preproduction machines, 35E1002, which is shown later in this chapter with the type of mount used on the production machines. *Copyright Harley-Davidson Michigan, Inc.*

ES was fitted with 0.050-inch compression plates that should have lowered both compression ratio and power. The E and EL were fitted with a 23-tooth engine sprocket, a 37-tooth clutch sprocket, a 22-tooth transmission sprocket, and a 51-tooth rear sprocket, for an overall ratio of 1:3.73. On the ES with a four-speed transmission, the engine sprocket was changed to 20 teeth, for an overall ratio of 1:4.29. On the ES with the three-speed-with-reverse transmission, the engine sprocket was changed to 19 teeth, for an overall ratio of 1:4.51.

A four-speed transmission was standard, but a three-speed transmission could be ordered at no additional cost. For $5.00 extra, the three-speed-with-reverse transmission could be ordered. Early in the year, only standard handlebars

RIGHT: A 1936 EL that was repainted, chromed, and accessorized by its owners over the years. It is now owned by Jeff Coffman of Jeff's American Classics of Dundee, Oregon.

A close-up of the 1936-only shifter gate showing the shift pattern: 1-neutral-2-3-4, from front to back. For 1936 only, the shifter-gate slot is smooth sided, without notched detents to hold the lever in gear position. Rather, the tapered top of the spring-loaded plunger shown through the slot, around the shift lever's shaft, engages scallops along the edge of the slot. With this gate, the shifting motion is straight forward or back, no jockeying to the side to clear notched detents.

were available, but Speedster handlebars became available March 3, 1936.

Two option groups for solo machines were offered. The Standard Solo Group included the front safety guard, steering damper, ride control, and jiffy stand; it listed for $14.00. The Deluxe Solo Group included all the items in the standard group, plus the Chrome Plate Group (chrome handlebars, headlamp, kickstarter lever, muffler [but not the muffler clamps], exhaust pipes, clutch inspection cover, and safety guard), fender lamp, stop light, dice shift knob, foot-pedal rubbers, and saddlebags and hangers; it listed for $34.50.

Styling

Production 1936 61 OHVs carried on the same sleek styling that had been so obviously right on the 1935-serialed 61 shown at the dealers' convention. The new machine featured smooth, streamlined, almost organic lines from front to rear. Perhaps more than any other feature, the styling of the 1936 61 shaped the future of Harley-Davidson. For model year 1937, all H-D models from the 45 to the 80 were updated to look like the 61. The basics of this style carried through on all H-D Big Twins through the mid-1960s. It became more and more muted in the 1970s, but was revived almost in its entirety on the Heritage Softails beginning in the mid-1980s, and helped spark a second renaissance for the company. In the 1990s, the styling cues set on the 1936 61, which proved once again so popular for Harley-Davidson, were also imitated by the Japanese manufacturers on their increasingly Harley-like and popular big cruisers.

Gas Tanks

The twin, saddle-type gas tanks were the most obvious styling improvement on the new OHV models. Gone were the boxy lines of the earlier Harley-Davidson Big Twin tanks,

replaced by rounded, teardrop-shaped tanks that carried through the tapered line traced by the frame from steering head to rear axle. Each tank has its own separate filler cap and petcock. The left tank holds 2.0 gallons and the right holds 1.75 gallons. Switched to the down position, the petcocks retain a reserve capacity of 1/2 gallon. Switched to the up position, the reserve capacity is available to take the rider those last miles to the next gas station. The left gas tank has a mounting lug for the gearshift-lever pivot and threaded holes for the shifter gate.

Instrument Panel

Perched on top of the tanks is a stylish, all-new instrument panel that encloses the speedometer, ammeter, oil-pressure indicator, and ignition switch. The shape of the panel suggests the shape of a skull—with the large round opening at the front for the speedometer being the cranium, the two gracefully curved apertures for the ammeter and oil-pressure indicator being the eye sockets, and the round opening for the ignition switch being the mouth. It has thus been nicknamed the "skull-face" instrument panel among enthusiasts. The panel was painted black on the outside and white on the inside.

Skull-face-style panels were used on 1936–1938 61s, but the 1936 panel is unique in that it lacks a hole for a speedometer-light switch (a small hole just aft of the ignition-switch hole) that appears on the 1937 and 1938 panels. If a speedometer with a trip odometer was originally fitted, a hole was drilled in the right side of the panel for the trip-odometer reset stem. A rubber grommet was fitted over the stem to keep moisture from getting inside the panel through the reset-stem hole.

The 1936 61 was the first Harley-Davidson Big Twin to be fitted with a speedometer as standard equipment, and the speedometer was given pride of place at the front of the instrument panel. Built by Stewart-Warner, the 100-mile-per-hour speedometer has a brass face plate with etched silver plating for a background. The numerals 10 through 100 are in black, with long hash marks for the numerals and short hash marks in between for the intermediate 5-mile-per-hour positions, also in black. A black pointer revolves around a pivot in the center of the face. The odometer window is forward of the pointer pivot. On tripmeter-equipped speedometers, the main odometer window displays five digits, all for miles and none for tenth miles, in black numerals on a white background. On nontripmeter speedometers, the odometer displays six digits, five for miles (in black numerals on a white background) and one for tenth miles (in red numerals on a white background). The tripmeter window (if a trip odometer was fitted) is aft of the pivot and displays three digits, two for miles (in black on a white background) and one for tenth miles (in red on a white background). A black H-D bar and shield is aft of the odometer. The glass is flat, and the bezel around the glass is chrome plated.

The 100-mile-per-hour speedometer was a 1936-only part for the 61. In stock form, a well-tuned 61 could just about bury the speedometer needle, so for 1937 the speedometer face was revised to read to 120 miles per hour.

The ammeter and oil-pressure indicator are situated aft of the speedometer, the ammeter to the left and the oil

Another view of Dave Banks' 36EL1374. Banks has owned his bike since the early 1970s. While others were still chopping such early machines, Banks restored his in 1974 and stuck it away in his basement. Twenty years later he pulled it out and began riding it. Today, it shows some wear and dirt from use, but is still in great shape. The chrome-plated exhaust was available as part of the Deluxe Solo Group, but the muffler hangers were still painted black when they left the factory. It also has the later, one-piece front safety bar. Early machines such as this one were probably fitted at the factory with the three-piece safety bar.

indicator to the right. The ammeter's needle indicated charge or discharge rates from plus-15 to minus-15 amperes. The oil-pressure indicator was little more than a mechanical version of the "idiot lights" that later became common. When the engine was off or oil pressure fell below 4 psi, the word "OFF" became visible through the indicator window. When oil pressure was above 4 psi, the word "RUN" became visible. The indicator was operated by a small oil line that connected the indicator to the oil pump. The ammeter and mechanical oil-pressure indicator were used on 1936–1937 61s.

Aft of the indicators is the ignition switch, which is key-lockable and has four positions: left position routes electricity to the front-fender lamp and taillamp, the center position is off, the next position to the right is for running the bike without lights, and the rightmost position is for normal operation with lights on.

Fenders

The swoopy, valanced front and rear fenders on the 1936 61 are two of the few example of parts carried over onto the new model from the Series V side-valve Big Twins. These fenders, first introduced on the 1934 models, look more at home on the sleek new 61 than they do on the Series V machines, which makes one wonder whether they were conceived as part of the overall design effort for the 61. Both fenders were constructed by spot-welding side valances to the center crown piece.

The front fender is attached to the fork by two braces on each side. Front and rear braces are riveted to a common brace clip on each side, and the brace clip bolts to the fork's rigid legs. Each brace is formed from a single piece of 5/8-inch wide steel, with the center section riveted to the inside surface of the fender and the left and right legs extending down to the brace clips. The attachment of the brace to the fender is reinforced by a butterfly-shaped plate spot welded over the center of each brace and fender, on the bottom side of the fender. These reinforcements were used for 1936–1938. The rest of the fender was carried over largely unchanged through the end of Knucklehead production (in 1939, stainless steel fender trim was added, and the braces were made wider in late 1946). The rear fender is hinged so that the rear section can be swung up and out of the way for easier tire changes.

Carman Brown's EL, one of the first 20 built, was fitted with an early version of the left crankcase. Identifying features of the early case include a small-diameter timing hole plugged with a straight-slot screw (just below the serial-number boss) and the lack of the small "eared" boss on each side of the crankcase's top stud (located just above the serial-number boss). This bike shines like new. It is one of the rare early Knuckleheads that still has the correct cup-type valve-spring covers. The rear exhaust cover is just visible at the right edge of the photograph.

Like the front fender, the rear fender has two fender braces on each side, both of which are riveted to a brace clip. The front brace is one piece, like those on the front fender, and is riveted to the underside of the fender and reinforced with a butterfly plate. It attaches to the fender just in front of the fender hinge. The rear brace consists of three pieces that form a detachable brace that can be unbolted to allow the hinged rear fender section to be swung up and out of the way.

The rear mount for the rear chainguard is unique to the 1936 61 (although a similar mount is used on the side-valve twins). The mount is riveted to the rear fender's left front brace. On 1937 and later 61 fenders, the mount was made part of a redesigned left-side brace clip.

Paint and Graphics

The paint and graphics on the 1936 61 OHV were nothing short of stunning. The gas tanks were painted a solid color, without panels, but with a contrasting pinstripe that curves gracefully around the Art Deco transfer on the side of each tank. The fender crowns were painted the same color as the tank, but the fender valances and braces were painted the color of the tank pinstripe. The valance panels wrapped around the front tip of the front fender and around the rear tip of the rear fender. A pinstripe of the main color parallels the curve of the valance's lower edge, about an inch up from the edge. Some bikes shown in the black-and-white photos taken in 1935 and 1936 clearly show a second pinstripe that separates each fender's main section from its panel; others don't. Was the upper pinstripe painted on standard-paint bikes for the whole year or for only part of the year? Or only with certain color combinations? And what color was the upper pinstripe. Dave Minerva, owner of an original-paint 1936 61 in the Venetian Blue and Croydon Creme combination reports that the upper pinstripe is gold on his bike.

Standard 1936 color choices were Sherwood Green with silver panels and wheel rims, Teak Red with black panels and red rims, Dusk Gray with Royal Buff panels and rims, Venetian Blue with Croydon Cream panels and rims, and maroon with Nile Green panels and rims. If one of these fetching color combinations didn't appeal to the buyer, custom colors were also available.

Though the order blanks don't list the option of custom colors, the dealers were well informed that just about any combination of colors and designs was available for the asking. The January 27, 1936, dealer bulletin featured the headline, "Please be explicit about special color specifications!" The accompanying text suggested that dealers describe thoroughly or even send a sketch for any special panels, striping, lettering, or designs the customer desired on his or her new machine.

Photos from the period show a wide variety of paint schemes on new machines, suggesting that many buyers took advantage of the option. Some were all white, with just the pinstripes on the tank and panels. Others had solid-color tanks (without even the pinstriping) or VL-style, thick tank stripes (the February 1937 *The Motorcyclist* shows a photo of "Red" Wolverton's 1936 61 with these stripes). Other riders didn't care for the color-matched wheel rims and chose black-painted rims or even cadmium-plated ones. Surely there is enough documentable variety to give any Antique Motorcycle Club of America (AMCA) judge heartburn.

The Knucklehead Engine

The 1936 61 was more than just a styling exercise, however. It was a completely new motorcycle with features that were modern in almost every way—features that proved so functional that many are still in use on Harley Big Twins today. And most of these were in the motor.

The left side of Banks' EL shows that by the 374th bike off the line, the left crankcase had changed slightly compared to the one shown on Carman Brown's bike. Note the eared boss on each side of the top crankcase stud and the hex-headed plug in the larger-diameter timing hole. Rubber spark-plug caps are a functional update for a bike that is ridden frequently, but are not correct. Note the primer cups just to the inside of the V from each spark plug. A special gas cap was used in conjunction with these cups to prime the intake tract with fuel for cold starting. Banks' bike also retains the cup-type valve-spring covers.

Before we get heavily into the details of describing the individual parts and the myriad details of what changed during 1936, let's discuss the fundamental design of Harley-Davidson's new motor, little of which changed during that first year, and little of which has changed on H-D Big Twins to this day. The 1936 61 was powered by a 45-degree V-twin with a bore of 3 5/16 inches and a stroke of 3 1/2 inches, for a total displacement of 60.32 ci (988.6 cc). Harley-Davidson's copy writers naturally rounded this displacement up to 61 ci, the origin of its common name during the era. Almost every part in the engine was new, the result of the relentless pursuit of the two main design goals Bill Harley had set for it: OHV cylinder heads and a dry-sump, recirculating oil system. Neither overhead valves nor recirculating oil systems were revolutionary features on motorcycles then, but they represented a big, long-overdue step forward for Harley-Davidson in 1936. Since these features drove the overall design of the new motor, let's examine them first.

Harley's OHV System

Overhead valves had become common on British and European road bikes such as those built by Ariel, BMW, Brough, Douglas, Matchless, Triumph, and others in the late 1920s and early 1930s. These companies had switched to the new system because overhead valves provide a straighter path into the engine for the fuel-air mixture supplied by the carburetor and a straighter path out of the engine for the spent exhaust gasses. This results in higher volumetric efficiency, producing greater engine power from a given engine displacement.

Overhead valves had even been tried on American machines before 1936, but mostly on limited production racing iron built by Cyclone, Indian, and even Harley-Davidson. Harley also had used overhead valves on some of their small singles, but overhead valves were strangely absent from the big American twins until the debut of the 1936 61, because this greater efficiency came at the price of greater complexity, which meant greater manufacturing expense and more potential for problems. The OHV system Harley-Davidson chose—two valves per cylinder, operated by a train of rockers, pushrods, and a cam mounted in the crankcase—seems pretty low-tech by today's standards, but the system was thoroughly modern for 1936.

Cylinder Heads

The 1936 61's cylinder heads are castiron and are virtual mirror images of each other, with the intake ports of each pointing to the center of the V formed by the cylinders and the exhaust ports pointing out from the V. The intake ports are fitted with a removable intake nipple that threads into the intake port and is locked in place with a rivet. The outer portion of each nipple is also threaded, and the nuts that secure the intake manifold to each head thread onto this portion of the nipple. The exhaust header pipes slip inside a flange in the exhaust port.

The combustion chambers are hemispherical (a configuration later made famous on the high-performance Chrysler "Hemi" engines of the 1950s and 1960s). Each head carries two overhead valves set at an included valve angle of 90 degrees. Valve seats and guides are replaceable. On the left side of each head is the spark-plug hole. Also on the left side of the head, but on the underside of the lowest cooling fin, is the casting number 119-35 (front head) or 119-352 (rear head). On at least some of the 1935-serialed OHV motors, and possibly some of the very-early-1936 cylinder heads, the casting numbers were raised from the surface of the fin; on later heads, the numbers were recessed into the fin.

An air-brushed photo of 35E1002 shows the three-piece front safety guard fitted to early 1936 61s. The guard consisted of a center top mount and two side loops that clamped at the top to the center mount and at the bottom to the sidecar lugs on the frame. Obviously, this made the rider choose between a safety guard or a sidecar. A new safety guard was introduced during the 1936 production run that eliminated the either-or situation. Note that the small round covers on the end of the rocker shafts have been airbrushed over to show the large hex nuts that replaced the round tin covers early in the production year. Underneath the footboard, the 1936-only brake rod is visible. This rod has a 90-degree bend at each end, one inserted into a hole on the brake pedal and the other inserted into a hole on the crossover lever. For 1937, clevis ends were fitted to the rod. *Copyright Harley-Davidson Michigan, Inc.*

Each head and its attached rocker housing also provide support for the rocker-arm shafts. The right side of each head has three lugs for mounting the aluminum rocker housing that gives the engine its shape and provides the right-end support for the rocker-arm shafts. On the left side of each head, inboard of the spark-plug hole, is a 90-degree-V-shaped bracket that provides the support for the left end of the rocker-arm shafts. This bracket is integral with the head casting. Each "ear" of the bracket is rounded off on top and has a rocker shaft hole on the centerline near the rounded top.

The rocker shafts insert through the holes in the ears and are fixed in place by a nut. Each ear also has a short reinforcing rib rising vertically (with its axis at a 45-degree angle to the axis of the bracket) from the base of the V to about the height of the head's cooling fins.

To the rear of the spark-plug hole on the front cylinder head and to the front of the spark-plug hole on the rear head is a round, cast-in boss. The bosses were drilled and tapped for the optional primer cups, which seem to have been fitted to most low-serial-number 1936 61s but not to many later machines. Turning the primer cup opens a passage into the intake port, into which a shot of raw gas can be squirted from the special priming gun in the right gas tank cap to ease the task of starting the bike on a cold day. Primer cups on the early 61s were a curious holdover from the days of truly prim-

itive carburetors and seemed archaic and out of place on the sleek, new machine. If the primer cups were not ordered, the holes are plugged by screws.

Rocker Arms and Shafts

Each valve is opened by its own rocker arm and closed by a set of nested, coil-type valve springs. Each rocker arm rotates on its own shaft. The rocker-arm shafts are threaded at each end for fixing the shaft to the cylinder head and to the rocker box. Oil for the rockers and valves is carried by the rocker shafts through a ring groove around the shaft's right end, through a central passage that ends at an oil passage on the left end of the shaft, and along a groove on the bearing surface of the shaft.

Each rocker-arm casting has two arms, a pushrod arm and a valve arm, that are on opposite ends of the casting and point in opposite directions. The valve arm ends in a radiused pad, which is the surface that bears on the top of the valve stem. The pushrod arm's end is fitted with a replaceable pushrod ball socket, which is the surface that bears on the top of the push rod. The bottom end of the pushrod socket is a ball end that slips into the concave top end of the pushrod. Each rocker is drilled for an oil passage that picks up oil from the bearing surface and carries it to an opening near the valve-arm pad to lubricate the valve stem.

Valve-Spring Covers

The key to finally solving the oiling mess that had been the bane of the prototype and preproduction 61s was in integrating the two systems that defined the new motor: overhead valves and recirculating oiling. This was done through the design of a clever new cover for each valve that catches the oil from the valve gear and returns it to the engine.

Each cover consists of an upper and lower section. The lower cover is basically a stamped-steel cup with a center hole through which the valve guide is pressed to secure the lower cover to the head. A steel oil return line from each cover connects to the left side of the aluminum rocker housing. The upper part of the cover is a stamped cap with a slot through which the valve arm extends to push on and open the valve, and the cap is secured with a light press-fit over the lower cup. The rocker arms remained largely exposed because the valve-spring covers enclosed only the end of each rocker's valve arm.

After lubricating the rocker arms and valve stems, the oil drips into the lower valve-spring cover. A return line is attached at the low point of the cover, and the engine vacuum sucks the accumulated oil out the lower valve-spring covers and back into the engine.

These covers were the 1936 61's most controversial and trouble-prone feature. When the oil supply to the rocker mechanism was properly adjusted to supply just enough oil to keep the valves from squeaking, relatively little oil escaped the covers. Problems were mostly the result of dirt and water that were sucked into the covers through the valve-arm opening by the same engine vacuum that scavenged the oil out of the lower covers. This dirt and water accumulated inside the covers, mixing with the scavenged oil to form an abrasive sludge that contributed to valve-guide wear and was sucked into the engine, where it remained in circulation until the next oil change. Of more immediate concern, the sludge sometimes clogged the return line, so that oil filled the valve-spring cover and spilled over onto rider and machine.

Yes, the design of these covers was less than perfect, but they were certainly better than no covers at all. Remember, the covers were a last-minute fix, added some time after the preproduction models were built in late 1935 but before the bulk of production bikes were built. Consensus among 1936 61 enthusiasts seems to be that most production 61s were fitted with the valve-spring covers. This conclusion is based on the fact that no shop dopes have surfaced with retrofit instructions to add the covers to machines not fitted with them at the factory. Plus, the rave reviews that the dealers sent back to the factory about the very first production machines in late January and early February suggest that these machines had the covers. But others think the very first production machines lacked the covers. At least one of them has an early 61 that he claims was never fitted with the covers because none are on the machine and fins on the cylinder heads were not relieved to allow clearance for the covers. It is interesting to note that the break-in instructions for the 61, dated April 14, 1936, instructs riders to "put a few drops of oil around upper end of valve guides, particularly inlet valve guides." This implies that the valve-spring covers were not yet fitted at the time the instructions were written because the valve guides are not readily accessible when the covers are fitted, and the rear exhaust cover is almost impossible to remove when the motor is in the frame.

Which faction is right? Until definitive proof surfaces, I won't weigh in with an opinion on the issue, but I will say this: If the oft-repeated stories about the early 1936 61's propensities for coating the rider's legs with oil are true, they could just as easily be attributed to clogged return lines or maladjusted oiling as to a lack of valve-spring covers. I'll also cite a couple of documents that provide a "no-later-than" date for introduction of the covers. The first is *Shop Dope No. 140*, dated April 20, 1936, that mentions that "overoiling will be indicated by oil splashing from the spring covers." The second is the patent drawings for the oiling system submitted on William S. Harley's behalf by the law firm of Wheeler, Wheeler, and Wheeler on May 16, 1936. These drawings show valve-spring covers, but the covers are shaped differently than those on the production machines, and the oil return lines join together. The common line winds around one of the covers so that the viewer cannot see where it connects to the engine, but it appears *not* to attach to the rocker housing (where the return lines from the production covers are attached).

Rocker Housings

Besides being an integral part of the styling for the engine, the aluminum rocker housing attached to each head serves three purposes. First, it supports the rocker shafts. Second, it serves as the conduit that distributes oil to the two rocker assemblies. And third, it routes engine vacuum to the valve spring covers for use in returning the oil to the engine.

To support the right end of the rocker shafts, each rocker housing has two tunnels from the right side to the left side. At each end, the tunnel openings are about 1 1/2 inches. The left side of the rocker-tunnels are each sealed by a cork seal that is sandwiched between two steel washers and held in place by a spring clip that is inserted into a groove around the left side of the rocker tunnel opening. The right end of the shaft tunnel on the early-1936 61s is covered by a round, slightly domed chrome-plated cover that is fastened to the right end of the rocker shaft by a small center screw. These covers are the "knuckles" of the early rocker housings. On later 1936 61s, the round covers and the rope packing were replaced by large, chrome-plated nuts that threaded onto the exposed right end of the rocker shaft and a small seal.

Passages in each rocker housing route the oil to the rocker shafts. Oil return lines from the valve spring covers attach to the left side of the housing, which is drilled through to the pushrod tunnels that rise upward from the bottom of the housing. The return oil also provides the only lubrication to the pushrod ball sockets. The oiling and scavenging systems are discussed in more detail in their own section later in this chapter.

Prototype, preproduction, and possibly very-early production rocker housings are not drilled for the oil return lines because valve spring covers were not fitted. Early housings were

The kickstarter cover shown was introduced in mid-year, and has a boss for the transmission vent, just visible above the starter spring. The large shaft rising vertically out of the top of the cover connects to the clutch release lever on the outside of the case and to the release fingers on the inside of the case. The chrome-plated kickstarter arm was included in the Deluxe Solo Group or as part of the Special Chrome Plating package offered separately for $13.50. The cadmium-plated "hockey puck" inboard of the kicker arm is the stoplight switch, also included in the Deluxe Solo Group. A chain connected the switch's pull to the brake rod.

drilled for the fittings but the castings did not have bosses around the holes. Sometime during the production run, the castings were modified to include the bosses, and an air nipple was added to the front rocker housing. This air nipple is used to blow obstructions out of the return oil lines from the valve-spring covers and will be discussed in more detail later in the chapter.

Pushrods, Pushrod Covers, Tappets, and Tappet Blocks
The tappets, one per pushrod and valve, have a roller lower end that follows the eccentric surface of each camshaft lobe and converts the eccentricity into vertical motion. The tappets rise and fall within the two cast-iron tappet guide blocks (one per cylinder) attached to the top of the right crankcase to transfer the up-and-down motion to the pushrods, which then transfer the motion to the rocker arms.

Each pushrod is fully covered by a two-piece, telescoping pushrod cover with cork seals. The unflanged bottom of each lower cover nestles inside one of the ridged crowns of a tappet guide and rests on a cork seal. The flange at the top of each lower cover is fitted with another cork seal, a washer on top of the seal, a spring on top of the washer, and a spring cap on top of the spring. The lower end of the upper cover fits inside the spring cap and seal.

Each upper cover has a flange at its top end that slips inside a pushrod tunnel in the bottom of the rocker housing and is sealed with a cork washer. The upper and lower covers are prevented from telescoping together by a spring-cap retainer that bears against the flange at the top of the top cover and against the spring cap that rests atop the lower cover. When the retainer is removed, the upper cover can telescope inside the lower cover so that the adjuster screw on the tappet can be accessed during valve-lash adjustment.

The new OHV system wasn't perfect, and many parts of it changed that first year and in the years that followed. But the valve gear gave the 61 unprecedented performance for an American production twin. Even in its purposely mild state of tune, the OHV engine could propel the 61 to an honest 95 miles per hour. Unfortunately, it didn't remain the fastest American twin for long. That title was wrested from Harley's grasp by the 61-ci OHV Crocker V-twin that appeared later in 1936. While the high-priced Crocker didn't pose any real sales threat to Harley's 61 OHV (probably less than 20 Crockers were produced per year), it trounced the Harleys—and Indians, too—whenever they met.

But the superiority of the limited-production Crocker does not in any way diminish the importance of what Bill Harley and his design staff had accomplished. After all, the Crocker firm is long gone, while Harley-Davidson thrives, and the OHV configuration Harley uses in the 1990s has far more similarities to the configuration set on the 1936 61 than it does differences.

Pressure Oiling System
Like overhead valves, recirculating oil systems had been in use for many years before 1936, when the 61 OHV introduced the feature to the Harley line-up. Unlike overhead valves, recirculating oil systems had been common even in America. Harley's main competitor in the U.S. market, Indian, had introduced the feature on its big twin Chief in 1933—and Indian's advertisements and sales brochures often pointed to this feature as evidence of the superiority of machines, which no doubt fueled the competitive fires in the boardroom in Milwaukee. Although Harley was just playing catch-up with this feature, catch-up was all that was really needed because the OHV top-end of the motor put H-D in the technological lead against Indian, and Indian would not survive long enough to close the gap.

The recirculating oil system Bill Harley and his staff designed for the 61 is of the dry-sump type, meaning that the oil is stored in a separate tank and not in the engine's sump.

Dry-sump systems had been used on many other motorcycles, including Indian, but few of the period were as elegant as Harley's turned out to be.

Oil Tanks

One of the main problems for designers of motorcycle dry-sump systems had always been the location of the oil tank. The tank had to be accessible so the rider could check, add, and change the oil, but it also had to be close to the pump to reduce problems with routing vulnerable oil lines. It also had to be large enough to hold a usable oil supply. Some manufacturers had taken the easy way out and haphazardly hung the oil tank to a frame downtube or anywhere it would fit. These systems worked, but they tended to detract severely from the looks of the machine. Others, including Indian, had partitioned the fuel tank to hold the oil. This, too, performed acceptably, but the oil lines tended to be long and the oil tank's capacity came at the cost of fuel capacity.

The best dry-sump systems were on the British OHV models of the late 1920s and early 1930s, such as the Norton Model 18 and Sunbeam Model 90, which had their oil tanks under the seat, an area that was close to the rear of the engine. Bill Harley chose this location also.

What set Harley's design apart was the way it perfectly blended form and function. The 1-gallon oil tank on the 61 is U-shaped, with the open end of the U pointing to the rear. It is perfectly placed to deliver oil by the shortest route to the oil pump, but it also wraps around the battery, hiding the blocky battery from view, contributing to the rounded, streamlined, almost organic lines of the bike. This classic, functional styling cue still contributes to the "Harley look" on such current models as the Heritage Softail. During its development and first year, the Knucklehead oil tank evolved through at least four versions. The first version, apparently used on some of the prototypes and maybe a few other very early machines, has smooth top and bottom surfaces. It is also identified by one banjo-type fitting at the right rear for the oil feed line to the pump, two banjo-type fittings at the front for the oil return and vent lines, a filtering screen at the front of the right lobe of the oil tank, and a plugged hole on each side of the tank. The fittings and plugs are welded in place.

The second type of oil tank, used on some early machines, is just like the first, except that it does not have the welded-in plugs on the sides. Later in the year, a third type was introduced. This tank differed from the second in that its top surface was embossed with reinforcements. Still later, the fourth type was introduced. The fourth type has the embossed top of the third type, but the banjo fittings are swaged on, not welded on. A decal with oil-change instructions was attached to the front right side of the oil tank, below the oil return and vent fittings. These oil tanks and the oil-change decal were used only for 1936. At least, some of the 1936 61s were fitted with a dipstick that differs slightly from dipsticks used in later years. The 1936-only dipstick has a longer ridge, which runs from edge to edge.

This view shows the mounts for the updated safety guard and the sidecar lugs on the frame. Note the accessory tire pump mounted along the frame's right downtube.

Oil Pumps

The all-new, gear-type pump on the 1936 61 is the heart of the recirculating oil system. The pump is contained in a separate housing attached to the outside of the rear end of the gear case and is really two pumps in one—a pressure-feed pump to force oil throughout the engine, and a scavenge pump to return oil to the oil tank. The oil pump body and cover are cast iron and are painted silver.

The oil tank is mounted higher than the oil pump, so gravity assists the pump in drawing oil through a feed line from the back of the oil tank to the oil pump inlet, where the gears of the pump force it to the pressure side of the pump. When oil pressure reaches about 1.5 psi, the oil unseats the ball in the check valve (which prevents oil from flowing out of the oil tank and into the crankcase while the engine is shut off) and flows to a branched passage. One branch leads to the oil-feed passages in the crankcase, and the other to the maximum pressure regulating valve (which remains closed until the oil pressure reaches about 15 psi, when the oil unseats the valve's check ball and bleeds off past the valve to the gear case). The oil pump also directs a small amount of oil to lubricate the primary chain and to actuate the oil-pressure indicator on the instrument panel.

Bottom-End Oiling

Oil to the lower end is forced through passages in the pinion gear shaft to lubricate the gear-shaft bearings and lower connecting-rod bearings. After lubricating these parts, the oil is slung around by the spinning flywheels, forming an air-oil mist that helps lubricate the cylinder walls, the wrist pins, and the left main bearing.

The flywheels spin clockwise (when viewed from the right side of the powerplant), so flywheel action tends to sling a lot of lubricant on the rear cylinder's walls but little on the front cylinder's walls. To counteract this tendency, H-D engineers used a system of baffles to create more vacuum under the front piston when it rises (which draws in more of the air-oil mist to lubricate the cylinder) and to partially block the spray of oil to the rear cylinder. The front cylinder baffle plate completely covers the opening to the cylinder, except for a slot for the connecting rod. The rear cylinder's baffle covers only the rear half of the opening, again, except for a connecting-rod slot. This basic configuration for cylinder oiling was used through 1939.

Top-End Oiling

Oil to the top end is carried from the gear case by an external, tubular-steel oil line that bends inward toward the cylinders, hiding itself behind the carburetor. The oil line branches to a fitting on each rocker housing, near the intake rocker shaft cover. In each cylinder head, the oil flows through a passage in the rocker housing and to the rocker-arm shafts. A groove running down the shaft distributes oil along its length to lubricate the rocker bearing. The hollow rocker shaft also carries oil to a passage in the rocker's valve arm to lubricate the valve pads and valve guides.

The oil supply to the valves can be adjusted after removing the large, chrome, domed "knuckle" covers or later chromed "knuckle" nuts to expose the right ends of the rocker shafts. Oil supply is increased by turning the end of the rocker shaft toward the valve-arm side of each rocker (that is, clockwise for the front cylinder exhaust and rear cylinder intake valve shafts, or counterclockwise for the front cylinder intake and rear cylinder exhaust valve shafts) or reduced by turning it

toward the pushrod arm. After lubricating the rocker shafts, the oil bleeds out the valve-arm end of the rocker arm (and the oil passage to the intake valve guide on some machines).

"Direct Oil Injection" to the Combustion Chambers

Sometime early in the production run, the rocker-arm shaft support brackets on the cylinder heads were drilled with an oil passage to the intake valve guides. The special intake guide fitted to these machines has a groove all the way around its outside diameter and is cross-drilled to distribute the oil to the valve stem. This was apparently an attempt to ensure that the valve guides got enough lubrication even when the overhead oilers were adjusted for the lowest possible oil flow to keep oil spray to a minimum. As you can probably imagine, this was an ill-fated modification because engine vacuum sucked the oil right into the combustion chambers to foul the plugs and burn into billowing clouds of blue smoke. Ever light on their feet, Harley-Davidson stopped drilling the passages on new machines after the problem was discovered, sometime during the middle of the production run.

Scavenging and Breathing Systems

The heart of the 61 OHV engine breather system is the rotary breather valve in the gear case, which allows crankcase pressure to escape and routes engine vacuum where needed to help scavenge oil. The heart of the scavenge system is the scavenge section of the oil pump, which draws scavenged oil out of the gear case and returns it to the oil tank.

The geared rotary breather valve is driven at crankshaft speed by the cam gear and is timed to open a passage from the crankcase to the gear case each time the pistons are on their down stroke. Crankcase pressure blows accumulated oil and the air-oil mist created by all the rapidly moving parts from the crankcase through the breather-valve opening and into the gear case, where the oil mist lubricates the gears. Early engines were fitted with a breather that had a flat screen held to the valve with a stamped metal bracket. Later engines were fitted with an updated valve with a tubular screen that was much more likely to stay in place than was the flat screen.

Crankcase air is vented out of the main gear-case chamber through an integral breather pipe in the gear-case cover and into the breather oil trap chamber at the rear of the gear case. In this chamber, oil is separated from the crankcase air by a screen and separator in the breather oil trap. The air is then vented out of the chamber through a separate breather pipe that extends to the left through both crankcases and into the primary-chain housing. Air expelled into the primary chain case still is mixed with a minute amount of oil, and this air-oil mixture is deflected onto the chain by the slotted, domed head of the breather pipe.

On the pistons' upstroke, the rotary breather valve is timed to close the passage to the gear case and connect a passage from the crankcase to the pushrod tubes and another passage to the breather oil trap. Vacuum created by the rising pistons pulls oil from the valve-spring covers through the pushrod tubes and into the gear case. Vacuum also sucks out the oil from the breather oil trap into the gear case. Oil

This view of Brown's EL shows the round covers over the right ends of the rocker shafts. A center screw threaded into a hole in the rocker shaft's end and fixed the cover in place. Rope packing behind the cover sealed the end of the shaft. With the covers removed, the rocker shafts could be turned to increase or decrease oil supply to the rockers and intake valve guides. Also shown is the 1936-only slash-cut air-intake horn. This air horn (not a filter) attaches to the carburetor with two screws. Early-1936 carburetors have a two-hole mounting boss for the air horn, but later carburetors have a four-hole boss for the accessory round air cleaner, which attaches with four screws. The carburetor should be nickel-plated, and the removable cap at the bottom of the fuel strainer (shown just below the air horn) should have cross-hatched, rather than straight, knurling.

trapped in the gear case is sucked out of the case and returned to the oil tank by the oil pump's scavenge section.

Proper sealing of the pushrod covers is vital to keep out dirt and keep vacuum and return oil in. If any of the seals leak, vacuum will be lost, return oil will leak out, and dirt could be drawn in by vacuum. If the seals leak too much, the remaining vacuum will be too weak to pull oil out of the valve-spring covers and back into the engine.

The whole oiling-scavenging-breathing system did its job well, keeping the parts well lubricated and most of the oil within the engine. A patent application for the system was filed on May 16, 1936, with William S. Harley listed as the inventor. The patent for the system (number 2,111,242) was granted on March 15, 1938. Normal oil consumption on the new 61 varied between 200 and 400 miles per quart, which seems very poor by today's standards, but it was much better than the total-loss oil system of other Harleys.

Pistons and Piston Rings

The 1936 Knucklehead used conventional cam-ground, slotted, aluminum pistons. They were offered in two versions: high compression and medium compression. The high-compression pistons, fitted to the Model EL, have a high dome, giving a compression ratio of 6.5:1. Medium-compression pistons were fitted to Models E and ES and have a much flatter crown, giving a compression ratio of 5.66:1 (the Models ES are also fitted with compression plates, lowering their compression further, but the specifications do not say by how much). Medium-compression pistons were fitted in 1936 and 1937 only, according to the parts book. Thereafter, the medium-compression Models E and ES were fitted with high-compression pistons with compression plates to lower compression.

The front piston is fitted with two compression rings but no oil-control ring, whereas the rear piston is fitted with the two compression rings and an oil-control ring. This odd configuration was dictated by the aforementioned clockwise rotation of the flywheels, which slings a lot of oil onto the wall of the rear cylinder, but relatively little onto the wall of the front cylinder. Baffles described earlier in this chapter helped somewhat to even out the oiling to the cylinders.

Carburetor and Intake Manifolds

Fuel and air for the 1936 61 OHV motor were mixed by a side-draft-type 1-1/4-inch Linkert M-5 carburetor with a 1-1/6-inch, fixed venturi. These carburetors have three mounting holes on their manifold-end flange and two mounting holes in the air-horn flange. Sometime during the production run, a four-hole air-horn flange was introduced. The M-5 with two-hole air-horn flange was used for 1936 only. The M-5 with the four-hole flange was used from late 1936 through 1939.

On all 1936–1938 Linkert M-5 carburetors, the float bowl lacks a drain plug and has the number *7-64* in raised letters on the inside surface of the bowl. In 1939, a drain hole was added to the float bowl. M-5 carburetors were cast of bronze and were nickel plated, but the bodies were not polished before plating.

The Y-shaped intake-manifold assembly delivers the intake charge from the carburetor to each cylinder head's intake port. The manifold assembly includes the manifold, two large (2-inch) "plumber" nuts to attach the manifold to the each cylinder head's intake nipple, and two brass bushings to seal the plumber-nut connections. Incidentally, the plumber nuts and bushings were among the few parts the designers of the 61 borrowed from Harley's side-valve Big Twins. The time-proven design outlasted the Knucklehead itself, being used on Harley Big Twins into the 1950s. Some manifolds have a hole drilled in their underside. According to Chris Haynes, these holes were drilled for an after-market backfire valve. The valves were apparently of poor quality and eventually leaked, so they were replaced by a bolt to plug the hole. For 1936–1938, the manifold and plumber nuts were unpolished and nickel plated, matching the finish on the carburetor. For 1939, the manifold and nuts were cadmium plated.

The opening and closing of the carburetor's butterfly throttle valve is controlled by the spiral on the right handlebar, acting through a coil-protected control wire. (For those readers who are more familiar with modern motorcycles, a few terms need to be defined. The twistgrips on vintage Harleys are called "spirals." The two-piece cable that leads from the spiral consists of the "coil" and "control wire." The coil is a protective outer sheath consisting of a coil of wire covered in fabric. The control wire is a cable that slides freely inside the coil.) Harley-Davidson motorcycles had long been given a right-hand throttle, while some other motorcycle manufacturers, including Indian, favored left-hand throttles. For those who wanted them—mainly police officers, who wanted their right hand free, say to shoot their pistols at fleeing suspects—left-hand throttles were optional, and were usually sold on bikes with right-hand shift levers.

Air Intake Horn and Air Cleaner

Rounded at the front, squared off at the sides, and slash-cut at the rear, with three speed-lines embossed along its length, the standard air horn for the 1936 61 was another triumph of Art Deco styling. It was the mirror image of the air horn used on the 1935 side-valve Big Twins, which is further evidence that the 61 was originally planned as a 1935 model. The air horn was chrome plated and mounted to the carburetor with two screws. Although this horn was beautiful and distinctive, it wasn't really functional because it had no air-filter element. Worse, it was prone to rattling itself apart because the two mounting points were insufficient to hold it securely to the carburetor. This air horn was used only for 1936.

For those who wanted or needed an air filter, an optional 6-inch round air cleaner with a filter element was available for at least part of the production year. The cover is chrome-plated and has the H-D bar-and-shield stamped into the round face and an instruction plate riveted to the rim. The cover is fastened to the backing plate by four screws, and the backing plate is attached to the carburetor by four bolts. The copper-mesh air cleaner wraps around a mesh support welded to the steel backing plate. The backing plate is Parkerized. This air cleaner was also optional for 1937.

The early-1936 ignition timer used through serial number 1421. This and all Knucklehead timers use one set of points to time the spark to two cylinders. A two-lobed cam opens the points and both spark plugs fire each time the points break. Note the bolt head on the underside of the timer control strap lug, which differs from that shown on one of the other preproduction bikes, 35EL1003. The strap was updated again early in the production year. *Copyright Harley-Davidson Michigan, Inc.*

Cylinders

Cast iron was the standard material for motorcycle cylinders before World War II. It was inexpensive, easily cast into the complex shape of a finned cylinder, and easy to machine for a smooth cylinder bore. The material was also durable, so a liner of another material was not necessary, and its slight porosity allowed it to retain oil for good cylinder lubrication. Consequently, iron was the natural choice for the 1936 61 OHV's cylinders. Nearly 50 years passed before H-D would switch to aluminum cylinders on the Evolution Big Twin introduced in 1984.

The 61's cylinders were an all-new design. At the top, around the edge of the 3 5/16-inch bore, is a raised ridge that fits into a recess in the head to help seal the head gasket. Outside the ridge is the gasket surface with five head-bolt holes spaced around the circumference. A boss for each of the head bolts runs down from the gasket surface through the top four fins. Each head is clamped to the cylinder by bolts inserted from below, through drilled bosses, through holes in the head gasket, and into the threaded holes in the head.

The front hub of Dave Banks' EL showing cable-adjustment mechanism. Nuts threaded onto the control coil were used to adjust for slack in the cable. The operating lever, to which the cable attaches, has four round holes, as shown. The word "SOLO" is stamped between the closest-in two holes and the letters "SC" (for sidecar) between the two outer holes. This lever was used through 1941.

The cylinder bases are each held to the crankcases by four studs and nuts, with a base gasket between the cylinder base and the crankcase. External surfaces of the cylinders were painted black. The basic configuration of the 61's cylinders remained unchanged until 1940, when the head-bolt bosses were changed so that they passed through the top five fins.

Compression Plates

Additional tuning of compression ratio was offered for specialized uses. For motorcycles to be used with sidecars or under heavy load or extended low-speed operation, Harley-Davidson offered compression plates that could be used to create what is effectively medium-high and medium-low compression ratios. These plates are simple metal spacers, 0.050 inch thick, that are fitted under the cylinder base to raise the deck height, lowering compression

ratio. The 1936 and 1937 Model ES was fitted with medium-compression pistons and a compression plate beneath each cylinder. Starting in 1938, only the high-compression pistons were fitted, so compression plates were used with the high-compression pistons to create medium-compression engines.

The Bottom End

The 1936 61's lower end was far more conventional for its day than was the top end. Like those on the other Harley-Davidson Big Twins, the 61's connecting rods run on a common crankpin sandwiched between two flywheel halves, and a pair of mainshafts (one per flywheel half) serve as the axle

A left-side view of 35E1002. Although not as grimy as 35E1003 was shown to be, this machine shows signs of having been ridden—the dirt and wear on the white handgrips, rear sprocket, and oil tank. The oil tank on this bike also has the welded-in plug (the shiny spot near the top rim of the tank, about halfway back from the front of the tank). Look at the frontmost of the two stays for the rear fender. Note the riveted-on mount for the rear chain guard and how it differs from the one shown earlier on 35E1003. The type of mount shown here was used on the production machines for 1936 only. Note the three pinstripes on the safety guard—a thick one down the center and a thinner one on each side that end about halfway down the guard in an arrow-point flourish. The early-style steering damper knob is shown in profile ahead of the speedometer. It is the squared-off type used on most or all 1936 61s, but it lacks the welded-in reinforcement plate that seems to be present on the damper levers on most production bikes. *Copyright Harley-Davidson Michigan, Inc.*

about which the whole flywheel assembly rotates. Each flywheel half is 8 1/8 inches in diameter and has a tapered central hole for a center shaft and an off-center tapered hole for the crankpin. These flywheels were used on the 61s from 1936 through 1940.

The front cylinder rod's big end is "forked," and the rear cylinder rod's big end was designed to nestle inside the fork. Forked connecting rods were used on most V-twins of the era. Engine designers liked them because they are narrower than two connecting rods placed side-by-side, which then allows the engine designer to use a short, stiff crankpin. The only real disadvantage to the knife-and-fork arrangement is that it also puts both cylinders on the same centerline, to the detriment of rear-cylinder cooling. (If the big ends are placed side-by-side, the crankpin must be longer, but the front and rear cylinders could be offset, allowing a more direct flow of cooling air to the rear cylinder.) The tapered crankpin fits through the big-end bearings of the connecting rods, into the tapered, offset holes on the flywheel halves, and is secured on the outer side of each half by a crank-pin nut and lock plate. This basic arrangement was used through 1939.

The mainshaft from the left flywheel is called the "sprocket shaft." It is secured to the left flywheel on the inner side by the sprocket-shaft nut and lock plate. Supported by roller bearings in the left crankcase half, the sprocket shaft extends into the primary-chain case to drive the primary-chain sprocket. The sprocket then transfers engine power through a three-row primary chain to the clutch sprocket.

The center shaft from the right flywheel is called the "gear shaft." This shaft consists of two pieces, a stub shaft and a pinion shaft. The stub shaft is secured to the right flywheel on the inner side by the gear shaft nut and lock plate and extends through the roller bearings in the right crankcase. The pinion shaft, attached to the stub shaft by means of an eccentric tongue-and-groove joint, extends into the gear case on the right side of the engine to drive the oil pump, cam gear, breather valve, ignition circuit breaker, and generator. Attached directly to the gear shaft are two gears: the oil-pump drive gear and pinion gear.

The oil-pump drive gear is the innermost of the two gears and is machined into the shaft. It is a worm-type that meshes with a gear on the end of the oil pump drive shaft, to change the direction of drive 90-degrees toward the rear of the bike to turn the shaft for the oil pump. The shaft extends through the rear of the gear case to drive the two-section pump that is mounted at the rear of the crankcase on the right side.

The outer gear is the pinion gear, which is a separate piece that is press-fit onto the pinion shaft. This small diameter gear is comparatively wide. The width of the pinion gear allows it to mesh with two larger diameter gears that are thin and overlap each other—the cam gear (which is vertically above the pinion gear) and the intermediate gear (which is to the right of the pinion gear as viewed from the right side of the bike). The cam gear turns the single, four-lobed camshaft and drives the rotary crankcase breather valve gear that is aft of the cam gear.

The intermediate gear is driven off the inner portion of the pinion gear at half speed. Mounted on the intermediate gear's shaft, on the crankcase side, is another gear that drives (also at half speed) the ignition circuit breaker. (See the ignition discussion for more details.)

To the right of the intermediate gear is the idler gear. The idler gear transfers drive from the intermediate gear to the generator drive gear. The generator is mounted transversely on the front of the engine, its drive shaft extending into the gear case on the right side of the motorcycle and its end cover on the left. (See the charging system discussion for more details.)

"Lightning" Camshafts

The 1936 61 came with a new camshaft arrangement that was unlike the arrangement used on the side-valve Big Twins. The side-valves had a separate camshaft and gear for each valve because the flat valve angle and short pushrods of the side-valve engine prevented the use of angled-in pushrods necessary for a common camshaft. The long pushrods and 90-degree included valve angle of the new OHV engine allowed all four pushrods to be angled into a single four-lobed cam.

Besides the obvious benefits of reduced manufacturing cost and complexity, the single-cam arrangement ran quieter and gave more consistent and precise timing because only one gear was needed instead of four.

The cams fitted to the 1936 61 OHV are different from most that followed and have gained a reputation as being especially "hot." In later years, these cams were much sought after by savvy performance tuners who knew the cam's reputation and how to pick them out of the milk crates full of lesser cams at swap meets. These special cams are identified by the measures taken to lighten the cam gear—six holes and metal machined away on the front and back. References to these lightening measures and the performance offered by the cam resulted in the description "lightening" being misconstrued into a nickname for the cam: "Lightning."

Some sources report that at least three versions of this cam were offered in 1936. The cam fitted to the early 61s was reportedly so far advanced that the bikes were prone to backfiring while being kickstarted. Sports-oriented riders could overlook the occasional backfire because these cams gave great performance, especially at higher rpm. Later, the cam timing was reportedly retarded to reduce this tendency. Still later, some say, a third cam was released that had two sets of timing mark, one for solo machines and another for those equipped with a sidecar.

Crankcases

All unaltered 1936 61 OHV left engine cases have a cast-in baffle covering the rear half of the rear cylinder hole (except for the slot running fore and aft for the connecting rod), a full baffle covering the front cylinder hole (except for the con-rod slot), and the casting number 112-35 (in raised numbers) below the primary-cover boss. Early-1936 left cases have a small-diameter timing hole,

Carman Brown's 36EL is at least as shiny and beautiful as the day it left the factory. This view shows how sleek and slim a sports machine the first Knucklehead really was. In later years the basic design set in 1936 would gain much weight and girth, better suspension, and accessories—and would evolve into the classic American touring bike. Very few bikes Harley-Davidson has built in the last 60-odd years have equaled the looks of the first Knuckleheads.

which is usually plugged by a cad-plated, straight-slot screw, Later cases have a larger timing hole (plugged by a cad-plated bolt) and two small raised "ears" above the serial-number boss, one on each side of the hole for the top crankcase stud. This second style of left case remained in use through mid-1939.

Only one style of right crankcase was used in 1936. It has the baffles and the casting number 112-352 below the gear cover. This case was used through 1939.

"Line-boring" Numbers

At the start of engine assembly, each Knucklehead crankcase set was bolted together and the mainshaft holes were line-bored through both cases at once, ensuring that the holes were in good alignment. The matched set of cases were then each stamped with a "line-bore" number. The number consisted of two digits for the year and four digits to denote the engine's place in the production run, separated by a hyphen. For example, 36-1234 indicated that it was the 234th set of 61 cases line-bored in 1936. In later years, when production was

higher, five digits denoted the engine's place in the production run. The line-bore numbers seldom match the serial number because the line-bore numbers were applied at the start of assembly, whereas the serial numbers were applied near the end of final engine assembly. However, line-bore numbers and serial numbers seldom differ by more than 100 or so. The two-digit number apparently indicates the year the case was line-bored, which is not necessarily the model year of the motorcycle. For example, some 1937-serialed cases have line-bore numbers that begin with "36" because they were line-bored in 1936.

Gear-Case Covers

At least three different gear-case covers are known to have been used on 1936 61s. The earliest style is called a "notched" cover, in reference to the recessed notch at the rear end of the cover. Inside, this cover has a steel baffle riveted on to shield the inlet to the gear-case breather pipe that is cast into the cover. The rivets that secure the baffle often were leaded over at the factory, but the lead plugs work lose from the vibration and heating-and-cooling cycles of decades of use, so the rivets are often visible on the outside of the cover.

Later covers are "smooth," in that they lack the notch of the earlier covers. The first smooth covers still had the riveted-on baffle, and the rivets sometimes show on the outside of the cover. Still later, the gear cover casting was revised to feature a cast-in baffle. Rivets were not used on the last style of cover, and it was used on subsequent 61s through 1939.

Exhaust System

The 1936 61 was fitted with a two-into-one exhaust system consisting of a front header pipe, an S-pipe, a rear header pipe, and a muffler with an attached collector pipe. Exhaust gases flow from the front cylinder through the front header pipe, through the S-pipe, and to the front connection on the pipe. Gasses from the rear cylinder flow through the rear header pipe to the top connection on the muffler pipe.

The tubular muffler is 2 1/2 inches in diameter and has a pretty flamboyant fishtail at its back end. Photos of preproduction bike 35EL1002 show the name "Burgess Battery Co." in large, raised letters on the muffler's side. Apparently, the Burgess name was too conspicuous for Harley-Davidson's liking because the name was moved to the bottom of the muffler, in much smaller letters, on the mufflers fitted to the regular production machines.

All components of the standard exhaust were painted black, but a chrome-plated exhaust was available as part of the Chrome Plate Group. Even with chrome-plated mufflers and pipes, however, the black clamps were fitted.

Charging System

The 1936 Knucklehead's charging system was one of the few systems on the new machine that was carried over from Harley's earlier twins. The system consists of a generator, external generator cut-out relay, and a battery.

The generator is the Model 32E 6-volt DC unit with a rotating armature, two magnetic field coils (regulating and

The forks and horn were new designs for 1936 and contributed to the bikes' classic lines. The only damping on these spring forks was provided by the optional "ride control" plates shown on Dave Banks' bike. Ride control was just friction damping that could be adjusted by tightening or loosening the lower knob. Note the grease fitting pointing forward on the spring perch, above and to the side of the upper horn mount. One such fitting is on each side. The fittings were in this location from 1936 through 1938. In 1939, the grease fittings were moved to the side of the spring perch and point to the sides.

shunt) fixed to the generator case, and three brushes (positive, negative, and current-regulating) contacting the commutator. This generator is used without an external voltage regulator because the third brush regulates the current output. Moving the third brush toward the negative brush increases current output and moving it away decreases output.

Like the plumber nuts discussed earlier, the Model 32E worked so well that it was both borrowed from earlier Harleys and passed on to later Harleys, after the Knucklehead engine was discontinued. It was the standard generator for Harley-Davidson Big Twins from 1932 to1952.

For riders who needed more current than the Model 32E could supply—mainly police users with bike-mounted radios—Harley-Davidson offered an optional generator, the Model 32E2, that had longer armatures and fields to supply the extra current. The Model 32E2 generator is also a 6-volt,

three-brush design that is used with a cut-out relay but without a voltage regulator. It was optional for 1936–1938.

The external cut-out relay's function is to disconnect the generator from the rest of the electrical circuit until the voltage produced by the generator exceeds battery voltage (preventing the battery from discharging through the generator windings). This cut-out relay looks much like a voltage regulator and mounts just forward of the ignition circuit breaker, on the forward part of the right side of the motor. The cut-out relay was also carried over from earlier Harley-Davidson motorcycles (having been in service since 1932). This relay has two terminal posts and is correct for 1936 and 1937 Knuckleheads.

Ignition System

Magneto ignitions were common in the motorcycle industry in 1936, especially on serious sporting machines. Magnetos are simple, light, and relatively trouble free. But Harley-Davidson had abandoned the magneto on its Big Twins in favor of a point-and-ignition-coil system with a distributor, because coil-stoked ignitions give a hotter spark at start-up, and made the kick-start ritual more of a sure thing, especially in cold weather.

In 1927, the company again modified the ignition to create a curious style of coil ignition. By use of a clever concept known as "wasted spark," Harley created a coil ignition system that is nearly as simple as a magneto system because it requires just one set of breaker points and one coil to operate both cylinders (no distributor or second set of points and coil). The coil fires both spark plugs each time the points open, igniting the fuel-oil mixture in one cylinder and "wasting" the other spark on the burned gases being expelled from the other cylinder on its exhaust stroke. Naturally enough, Harley-Davidson chose to fit its new 61 with its wasted-spark system.

Looking much like an automotive distributor, the 61's ignition circuit breaker or timer is mounted to the right of the front cylinder. The timer's main functions are to open the breaker points, and to time the break so that it occurs at precisely the right instant. Inside the breaker cover is a set of breaker points, a two-lobed cam, and the condenser. The cam lobe for the front cylinder is narrower than the lobe for the rear cylinder. The timer shaft and cam are spun at half of the crankshaft speed (so the plugs fire every other stroke).

The ignition timer assembly fitted to the first 1936 61s was basically just a longer version of the timer fitted to the side-valve Big Twins. After motor number 1422 was built, a new timer was introduced. The new timer has larger diameter (45/64-inch, versus 5/8-inch) holes for the shaft. On both of these timer assemblies, the circuit-breaker wire feeds into the side of the assembly through a notch in the side of the timer base, and the wire connects to the top of a terminal on the base. Timers with the notched timer base were used only for 1936, because the timer was revised for 1937 to route the timer wire out through a hole in the timer housing, which made the wire less vulnerable to chafing.

A single twin-lead ignition coil generates the spark, and it is mounted on the motorcycle's left side, in front of the oil

Jeff Coffman's 36EL also has the notched gear cover, in addition to a lot of extra chrome and a red painted oil tank. In 1937, oil tanks were painted the main color of the bike and were fitted with the patent decal, as shown here.

tank. One spark-plug lead goes to the front spark plug and one to the rear plug, but both spark plugs fire each time the points are opened by the points cam. In greatly updated form, with electronic black boxes replacing the points and advance mechanism, the wasted-spark system is still in use on the 1990s Harleys.

Transmission and Shifter

Just as the OHV motor signaled the dawn of a new age for The Motor Company, so, too, did the new bike's transmission—an advanced, four-speed, constant-mesh design that was quieter, stronger, and more durable than the sliding-gear transmissions found on the competing Indian and foreign motorcycles. Although a constant-mesh transmission had been used on a few earlier 45-ci Harleys, the 1936 61 was the first Harley-Davidson Big Twin to use a constant-mesh transmission.

The all-new transmission was carried in its own housing separate from the engine, and this basic transmission proved to be one of the 1936 Knucklehead's most enduring features. In fact, it was passed on largely unchanged to all the Harley-Davidson Big Twins through 1964, except for those built during the 1939 model year when a curious new four-speed was used that was a hybrid of the constant-mesh and the older sliding-gear types. Optional transmissions included a three-speed and a three-speed with reverse.

Transmission Cases

The components of the new transmission were housed in at least two different transmission cases for 1936, neither of which had a cast-in support for the kickstarter side of the transmission. The early 1936 case has four frame mounting studs and is not drilled for the mounting holes for the countershaft end cap fitted to later cases. In mid-1936 H-D began drilling the transmission case for the four countershaft-end screws. The case was supported on the starter side by a bracket attached to the two lower studs for the starter cover and a bolt that butts against the lower frame tube. In late 1936, a new starter-side support bracket was introduced. More details on these mounts are provided later in this chapter.

Shifter and Linkage

In traditional Harley fashion, the new transmission was shifted through a gear-change lever that pivoted fore and aft on a bracket on the bottom of the left gas tank (although right-side shifters were optional). The gear-change lever moved within a shifter gate attached to the left gas tank. All the shifter parts were new for 1936. The gearshift lever was round in section, tapered from bottom to top, and featured a spring-loaded plunger near its top. The plunger mated with scallops in the underside of the gate to hold the gearshift lever in each gear's

The constant-mesh four-speed transmission was all-new for 1936 and would provide the basis for all Harley-Davidson Big Twin four-speeds to follow, except for the 1939 hybrid transmission with sliding second gear. Note the bolt and bracket that serves as the transmission support on the kickstarter end. The bolt extends down from the sheet-metal bracket, which is bolted to the lower two studs for the kickstarter cover. When properly adjusted, the bolt should just touch the lower frame tube. Problems arose when the bolt was over- or under-adjusted, so a new bracket and a mount on the frame was added late in the year. The new sheet-metal bracket was larger and stouter and extended down to butt against the frame mount, and the two were clamped together by a cap screw, providing a nonadjustable transmission mount on the kickstarter end. *Copyright Harley-Davidson Michigan, Inc.*

A rear view of the cutaway transmission showing the operating mechanism of the shift drum at top. At right are the kickstarter and clutch release mechanisms. Note the release fingers, the three-piece throw-out bearing, and the starter clutch. The three-piece, six-ball throw-out bearing had been carried over from the earlier singles and 45s. In mid-year, this bearing was replaced by a larger bearing with eight balls. Although the updated bearing was better, it still wasn't stout enough. It, too, was replaced, in late 1938, by an even larger bearing. *Copyright Harley-Davidson Michigan, Inc.*

position. From the rider's perspective, first gear was the farthest forward position, then came neutral, second gear, third gear, and fourth gear. To shift, the rider just pushed the lever forward or pulled it back. Both lever and gate are chrome-plated and were used only in 1936.

The shift lever is connected to the transmission's shifter shaft by a shifter rod with a clevis at the front end and a 90-degree bend at the back end. This shifter rod and clevis were cadmium plated and remained in use virtually unchanged through the end of the Knucklehead line in 1947.

Clutch

The transmission is connected to engine power via a conventional multiplate clutch and a primary chain. This clutch and drum proved to be nearly bullet-proof, able to handle much more than stock horsepower. Aside from a few changes to the discs, the assembly was carried forward onto the subsequent 61s through 1940.

The clutch disc pack consisted of five fiber friction discs, three flat steel discs, and one "humped" steel disc. The fiber discs have notches on their outer circumference that mate with the splines on the inside of the clutch drum. The flat steel discs have splines on their inner circumference that mate with the splines on the outside diameter of the clutch driving disc. Drive is transferred through splines on the inside of the clutch drum to the friction discs.

When the clutch is engaged, 10 clutch springs force the friction discs into contact with the steel discs, and the steel discs transfer the power to the clutch driving plate through their splined mating surface on the outside circumference of the driving disc's hub. And the driving plate transfers the power to the hub through another splined mating surface, this one on the inside circumference of the driving disc's hub.

The disc pack worked well under normal use, but under hard use or lots of stop-and-go driving, the discs sometimes would stick and drag. Even so they were carried over onto the early 1937 61s.

In traditional American practice, the clutch was foot operated by a pedal on the left side of the motorcycle. The pedal had toe and heel pads, the operation of which was the opposite of that used on cars and some other motorcycles, including Indian. Push down on the toe pedal, and the linkage would engage the clutch. Push down on the heel pad, and the linkage would disengage the clutch. The pedal is cadmium plated through about mid-1937 and is Parkerized thereafter. The foot-operated clutch-release mechanism was used on all Harley Big Twins through 1951.

The pedal connects to the transmission's clutch release lever by a rod that is threaded on the front for the clevis and is slightly flattened at the rear to slip into one of the two slots on the clutch release lever's end. The release lever is made of two pieces brazed together. The larger piece is a round rod with a dogleg bend, and the rod is flattened at the dogleg. The second piece is the right end, which has a square hole that mates with the release-lever stud, that extends through the kickstarter cover to attach to the release finger. This lever is cadmium plated and is used for 1936 and 1937.

The weak link in the 1936 61's clutch system was its throw-out bearing. Two different throw-out bearings were used in 1936 alone, and neither of these really proved satisfactory. On the first 1936 61s, Harley-Davidson reused the six-ball throwout bearing that was first used on the side-valve 45s introduced in late 1928. While the bearing was adequate for the loads imposed by the 45, it proved to be too weak to stand up to those of the 61, so it was replaced in midyear by a larger bearing with eight balls. This new bearing was used until mid-1938, when it was replaced with a still-larger bearing. And even this bearing wasn't stout enough, so it, too, was replaced for the 1939 model year.

Kickstarter Assembly

The 1936 61 was fitted with a conventional kickstarter assembly that includes a crank arm with pedal and return spring, a starter clutch, and gears to turn the transmission mainshaft and transfer the kickstarting force through the clutch to turn over the engine. The starter clutch disconnects the gears when the crank arm is in its rest position and again at the bottom of the stroke. Thus, if the rider pauses and holds the kicker arm at the bottom of the stroke, there is no danger of the engine kicking back through the crank.

The assembly is housed in the kickstarter cover on the transmission's right side. At least two covers were used during 1936 production, and the only significant difference between them is that the early 1936 cover has a milled flat for (but no boss for) the transmission vent tube, which is located above the starter-crank tunnel, while the late 1936 cover does have a cast-in boss for the vent. The later cover was also used on early 1937 61s.

On both covers, the starter, crank tunnel carries a one-piece bushing for the starter crank's shaft and the outer end of the tunnel is sealed by a cork washer held in a machined-in recess in the boss around the starter, crank tunnel. The tunnel boss is reinforced inside the cover by five ribs around the boss.

Early starters on four-speed transmissions used a 26-tooth starter-crank gear that meshed with a 14-tooth mainshaft starter gear. The gears were changed sometime early in the production run to 24 teeth on the starter-crank gear and 18 teeth on the mainshaft gear. This revised gearing was used on all four-speed transmissions through 1947 and on 1939-and-later three-speed and three-speed-with-reverse transmissions. The starters for 1936–1938 three-speed and three-speed with reverse transmissions use yet another gearing combination: 22 teeth on the crank gear and 18 teeth on the mainshaft gear.

Primary-Chain Housing

A two-piece guard covers the primary chain, keeping dirt off the chain and lubricant inside it. At least two different inner covers and three different outer covers were fitted at various times during the 1936 production cycle.

The inner cover used through mid-1936 lacks an oil drain hole because it is used in conjunction with an outer cover having a drain hole. Later 1936 inner covers are like the previous cover, except that a nipple for a drain pipe is added to the lower rear surface of the cover and two more reinforcement ribs are stamped in—a medium-length rib aft of the crankcase-breather-pipe hole and an even shorter one just aft that. All inner primary covers were painted black. Drain pipes were cadmium plated.

The first type of outer primary cover was probably fitted to only the preproduction 61s. It is unique in that it has a screw hole on each side of the primary-chain inspection-cover hole. The purpose of these holes is not known, but they probably fastened some sort of baffle. This outer cover also had a drain hole under the clutch derby.

The second type of primary cover used on the 61 is like the previous cover, except that it lacks the two screws fore and aft of the primary-chain inspection cover. This outer cover was first fitted sometime early in the production run, and may even have been fitted to the first production machines. It, too, has the drain hole. Some time during the production run, a third outer cover was introduced. The third 1936 outer cover was the same as the second type, except that the drain hole was omitted because this outer cover was used in combination with a new-type inner cover that had a fitting for a drain pipe. This third outer cover was then fitted to all subsequent Knuckleheads through 1940.

Outer primary covers were painted black. Standard chain inspection covers were chrome plated for 1936 and 1937, but were painted black for the following years (although plated covers were optional for most years). Standard clutch inspection covers were also painted black, but chrome-plated covers were part of the Chrome Finish Group for 1936 and 1937. Inner and outer covers are fastened together using 10 Parkerized fillister-head straight-slot screws.

Rear Chain Guard

Covering the rear drive chain is a stamped steel guard that is formed of two pieces riveted together near the front of the guard. It is attached at the front to a tab on the top of the inner primary cover and at the back to a mount riveted to the fender brace. This two-piece chain guard is correct on 1936–1938 61s. The guard is painted black.

Frame

The 1936 Knucklehead came with a frame as different and as modern as its engine. Previous Harley frames had all been single-downtube types that were really just descendants of turn-of-the-century bicycle frames. Single-downtube frames were light and easy to build, but they lacked the rigidity to handle higher weights and more horsepower. The new Knucklehead frame had twin downtubes that cradled the engine in a cage of chrome-moly tubing that stretched from the steering-head forging at the front to the axle-mount forgings at the rear. And its 28-degree steering-head angle gave a perfect balance of steering and stability with the stock 18-inch wheels and 4.00x18-inch tires. Unfortunately, the only rear suspension provided was the spring-mounted seat.

The top of each of the two main downtubes was single-butted to a slash-cut, larger diameter tube extending down

The two best-looking stock paint schemes on any of the Knuckleheads—1936 and 1939. The 1936 is owned by Dave Banks, and the 1939 by Ron Lacey. Note the chrome-plated clutch inspection cover on Banks' bike, which was included in the Chrome Plate Group, which was also part of the Deluxe Solo Group, as was the front fender lamp shown. Note the mount on the front stay for the rear fender. It is the type used beginning in 1937. The correct mount is a separate tab riveted to the back of the stay, about halfway up, as shown in the next photo.

from the steering head. From the butted joint, each tube sweeps down and back, around the engine and transmission, to join with the axle-mount forging for its side. The backbone tube is larger in diameter than the downtubes and angles down and back from the steering head to join with the seat-post tube.

Sidecar mounting loops are brazed to the front side of each down tube, and a mounting strap for the toolbox is brazed between the upper and lower tubes just forward of the right axle clip.

The engine mounts to the frame at three points: to a lug from the backbone tube, to a casting that bridges the down tubes underneath the front of the engine, and at the shelf-like rear motor mount attached to the front side of the seat-post tube. The transmission mounts to a plate that allows the transmission to be adjusted fore and aft to tighten or loosen the primary chain.

Sidecar Mounting Lugs

All production and pilot-production 1936 61 frames are thought to have come from the factory with sidecar mounting loops fastened to the front downtubes, but some of the

prototype and preproduction frames apparently did not have them, as shown in the disassembly photo of 35E1003. The sidecar lugs also served as the lower mounting point for the three-piece safety guards that were optional for most of the 1936 production year. Sidecar loops on early frames are brazed on, while those on some of the later frames appear to be welded on. When asked how the lugs on one of his frames was attached, Chris Haynes said they appeared to be tack-welded in place and brazed. It is possible that some very, very late 1936 61s were fitted with the updated frame for 1937 with the new-style sidecar-mount forgings that were introduced for that year. See chapter 2 for more details on this frame.

"Fifth" Transmission Mount

Anyone who has ever kicked over one of H-D's Big Twins knows first-hand how much force is transferred through the kick-starter's crank arm to the transmission, especially at the end of the stroke, when the rider's full weight bears down on a lever that is hard against its stop. The transmission on all 1936 61s had four studs for fastening it to the frame. On the kickstarter end of the transmission, unfortunately, the tranny case was not bolted to the frame. Rather, it was loosely supported by what seems to be another one of the under-thought quick fixes that were necessary to get the bike into production for 1936: a sheet-metal bracket was bolted to the kickstart cover and an adjustable support bolt extended down from the bracket to butt against the frame tube.

When properly adjusted, the bolt and bracket provide adequate auxiliary support to the four solid mounts on the transmission. But when improperly adjusted, a number of problems can result. If the bolt is not adjusted far enough down to contact the frame, kickstarting loads are transferred to the other transmission mounting studs and to the frame's transmission mounts, eventually resulting in studs torn loose from the transmission case and cracks forming near the mounts. If the bolt is adjusted too far out, it "cocks" the transmission so that the engine and the sprockets are no longer in line, causing binding and accelerated wear.

Harley-Davidson made the kickstarter-end support "idiot proof" late in the 1936 production run by introducing a "fifth," nonadjustable transmission mount to support that end of the transmission. The new mount consisted of a support pad brazed onto the frame and a revised support bracket that was more rectangular and stout, but which still attached to the lower studs on the kickstarter cover. The bottom of the bracket butted up against the top of the support pad on the frame and a cap screw clamped the two together, providing a fairly good fifth transmission mount.

The new mounting pad and bracket were carried over into 1937 production, but the bracket was eventually replaced by a cast-in lug on the revised transmission case that was introduced in mid-1937. Some authorities say that very, very late 1936 61s were fitted with the revised transmission case and thus do not use the bracket. This is unlikely, however, because the 1937 parts book states that the second type of bracket, part number 2263-36A, was used on the later 1936 61 and "first 1937 — 61, 74, & 80 twins."

Frame Cracking

In keeping with the sporting nature of the machine, the 1936 61's frame was made as light as possible. The main tubes are 7/8-inch diameter, which, it turned out, were too light. Because of this, the frames were prone to cracking at the seat post, the transmission mount, and on the left rear stay when the machines were ridden hard—especially off-road, as riders of the day often did. Cracks were fixed by welding the broken pieces, either at a dealership or at the factory. If the work was done at the factory, a number was often stamped in the reinforcement webbing behind the seat post.

When a sidecar was fitted, the front downtubes often cracked from the extra torsional strain transferred to the tubes through the sidecar mounting lugs. Anecdotal evidence exists that a fix for the latter problem was sometimes performed at the factory by brazing in a longer slash-cut reinforcement on the downtubes. The reinforcement on these frames extends far below the normal slash-cut joint, sometimes to a point just above the sidecar mounts. At least one example exists of a frame that

was apparently fitted with the longer reinforcements at the time the frame was built, as this frame shows no sign of modification. Were these frames built for the ES models for sidecar use? Or for the later ESs? Future research may supply the answer.

The real fix for the problems with frames cracking came in 1937, when a new frame was introduced that was heavier duty all around. Some authorities say that the new frame was fitted to the very last 1936 61s and they cite the fact that many 1936 61 engines reside in these frames today (including the 1936 61 in the Harley-Davidson collection) as proof. Since no documentation exists to prove conclusively when the new frame was first fitted, the most I can offer is an opinion: Some very, very late 1936 61s may have come with the 1937 frame, but more likely the 1936 engines that are in these frames are there because the original cracked frame was replaced under warranty with the updated frame or because the owner upgraded the bike at a later date when it cracked or was damaged in an accident. It is very unlikely that Harley-Davidson stocked the trouble-prone 1936 frame as a replacement part.

Tool Boxes

The 1936 61 was fitted with a toolbox that is similar to but not exactly the same as the one fitted to the side-valve models. It mounts to a bracket on the right side of the motorcycle. The box is rectangular and mounts so that the long dimension is vertical. Its cover is held closed by a keyed lock.

Box and cover are painted black and a Harley-Davidson patent decal is attached to the cover. This rectangular toolbox is correct for 1936–1939 61s.

Forks and Handlebars

The new forks on the 1936 Knucklehead were leading link, spring-suspended forks with about 2 inches of travel. They differed little in concept from the forks on previous Harley Big Twins, but they were a bit stouter. Externally, the main difference was that the legs of the rigid fork on the new 61 look smoother and more streamlined because they were made of extruded, oval-section tubing, rather than of the drop-forged I-beams that the forks on the side-valve Big twins were made of.

The 1936 61's forks had no built-in damping, but optional friction plates, called "ride control," could be ordered. These plates, one on each side of the fork, could be tightened or loosened for more or less friction, much like the steering dampers of the day. On the 1936–1937 61's ride control, the adjusting knob was on the right side. On later machines, the adjusting knob was on the left side.

Only minor changes were made to these forks from 1936 to mid-1946, when they were replaced by the new "offset" springer forks. Distinguishing features of the early forks include two forward-facing grease fittings on the front of the spring-perch forging, and narrow, unreinforced mounting tabs for the front fender. The grease fittings remained in this location until they were moved to the outside left and right edges of the spring perch in 1939, so that the fittings point out to the sides. The narrow fender tabs were used through 1937, but for 1937 they were reinforced by a plate spot-welded underneath each.

Handlebars and Hand Controls

The 1936 61's handlebars were also new, to fit the new fork. The left and right bars are brazed to a center forging that has a center hole and two smaller-diameter flanking holes, into which the tops of the fork's rigid-leg tubes slip. Pinch bolts clamp the forging around the fork tubes. At the start of the model year, only the Standard bars were available, but the March 3, 1936, dealer news bulletin announced the availability of new, Speedster bars for the sport-oriented 61 rider. According to the bulletin, "The rider using them leans forward just a little and presents a race-like, speeding appearance." Speedster bars were available in place of the standard bars for no extra cost after this date. Bars were painted black unless the Deluxe Solo Group or Chrome Plate Group was ordered, in which case they were chrome plated.

The inner diameter of each bar end is threaded for a screw that retains the throttle spiral on the right and spark-control spiral on the left. The outer portion of the spirals show a 2 3/8-inch-wide chrome band inboard of the rubber grip. Correct grips swell in the midsection and have a pattern of ridges running the length of the grip. Standard grips were white rubber, but black grips were optional. Throttle and spark-control coils and control wires are routed through the bars and emerge from holes in the bosses near the ends of the handlebar's center forging. These spirals and grips are correct for 1936–1942.

The left bar also has a headlight dimmer switch, a horn switch, and the front-brake hand lever and bracket. The brake hand lever assembly consists of an S-shaped, chrome-plated steel lever and a Parkerized lever bracket and clamp bracket. This hand lever and bracket were used from 1936 through 1940.

Fork Top Plate

On at least the early-1936 61, the chrome-plated fork top plate has four 13/64-inch holes in it. Unfortunately, no one has been able to uncover their intended purpose. Later in the year (or possibly at the start of 1937 production?) this top plate was replaced by a stainless steel plate that lacks the holes.

Safety Guards

Two different optional front safety guards were fitted to 1936 61s. Early guards were made of three pieces—the top center clamp/mount and the two side loops. The top end of each loop slips into the center piece, and bolts are tightened to clamp the three pieces into a unit. The guard attaches at the top to the motorcycle's frame and at the bottom to the sidecar mounting lugs. Thus, a rider had to choose between having a sidecar attached or having a safety guard. The guard is painted black. Some photos show that the guards were pinstriped, but others show that they were not, so the pinstripes may have been an early-season feature. I have been able to locate only one unrestored machine that has pinstripes on the guard. Its owner reports that it has two stripes on each loop and that they are gold. These stripes may be original or they may have been added at a later date.

Some time during the production year (possibly coinciding with the introduction of the LE sidecar, which was first ready to ship on March 16, 1936, according to a dealer news bulletin), the three-piece guard was replaced by a new one-piece guard with revised lower mounts that attached to the footboard mounts. This arrangement freed up the sidecar mounting lugs so that a sidecar and a safety guard could be mounted simultaneously. The four bends in the guard are symmetrical, giving it a squared-off, boxy look that kind of clashes with the lines of the bike and limits cornering clearance. The new safety guard was also painted black, but was probably not pinstriped. This new guard was optional on 61s through 1938.

Lights and Horn

The Cycle-Ray headlight is fitted with a prefocused 21/32-candlepower bulb and separate reflector and lens. This lamp is identified by the names "Cycle-Ray" and "Guide" inside a circle stamped on the outside at the rear of the steel bucket and "Cycle-Ray" and "Made in the U.S.A." raised out of the face of the glass lens casting. The standard steel bucket is painted black for all years (but chrome-plated buckets were available as part of the Chrome Plate Group) and the lens doors are chrome plated for all but 1943 to mid-1946 models. The headlamp mounted to a bracket that is bolted to the headlamp lugs on the fork's rigid-leg's spring perch and to the handlebar center section.

The taillight is the "beehive" style that had been introduced on the 1935 Big Twins. The taillamp assembly includes a stamped-steel bracket with integral license-plate bracket, a stamped-steel lens bucket, and a red glass lens. The bracket is painted black, and the bucket is chrome plated. This taillight is correct for 1936–1938 61s.

The horn was a new part for 1936. It is a Delco-Remy Model 16 horn with winged-face cover and bolt-on brackets. The horn body is painted black, and the cover is chrome plated. A separate bracket attaches the horn to the headlight mount so that the horn rides underneath the headlight. This horn is correct for 1936–1941 Knuckleheads.

Although these 6-volt lights and horn are anemic by today's standards, they were as good as any of the day, and if a rider needed any more light, the optional Little King or Little Beauty spotlights were available. These accessory lights mounted to a crossbar on the handlebars and were listed at retail prices of $9.75–$11.75 for the Little Kings or $11.50–$13.50 for the Little Beauties (prices depending on which order blank was in effect at the time of order).

Wheels and Brakes

The Knucklehead was introduced when tall, narrow wheels and tires were still fashionable on American motorcycles, and the Knucklehead was still in production when fashion switched to fatter, softer-riding tires.

The first Knucklehead's rims were 2.15x18 inches, stamped steel, laced with cadmium-plated spokes, and fitted with 4.00x18-inch tires. Front and rear wheels and hubs are identical and interchangeable once the brake and drive parts are detached and interchanged.

The 1936's star hub has a step on the inside surface of the brake-side flange. These "stepped" hubs were used through

Carman Brown's 36EL. Note the correct 1936-only mount for the rear chain guard on the frontmost fender stay. Also note how the pinstripe angles forward and down at the front, paralleling the line of the fender's chain-guard recess.

1938 and turn on roller bearings. The brake-side flange is stamped steel. The hub star cover used on the 1936 61 was used only that year on the Knucklehead. The cover has two small, square holes 180 degrees apart, near the axle opening. These holes were omitted from the star covers used on 1937-and-later Knuckleheads. The cover was cadmium plated on 1936 and some 1937 Knuckleheads.

For 1936, the wheel rims were painted the color of the fender panels (except when the color scheme was Teak Red with black tank panels—then the rims were painted red). Cadmium-plated or black-enameled rims were optional that first year. Hubs were painted black.

The 1936 Knucklehead was fitted with front and rear mechanically actuated, internal-expanding brakes with two shoes each. Both brake drums are 7-1/4-inch inside diameter and are made of pressed steel. Upper and lower brake shoes are lined with an asbestos material and are interchangeable. The brake drum is attached to the hub by five lug bolts. For at least part of the 1936 production year, the lug nuts were drilled with a "safety-wire" hole. The holes may have been a response to all the problems experienced with the 1935 45 "demountable" rear wheel and brake hub, which were almost identical to those used on the 61. According to *Shop Dope No. 123* (dated March 15, 1935), "Demountable rear wheel clamp screws must be securely

tightened two or three times within the first few hundred miles after a machine goes in service." Lug nuts were probably not safety wired at the factory, but a dealer or owner who experienced problems with lugs that repeatedly loosened could wire them if necessary.

The front brake on the 1936 61 was a new unit designed for the bike's new spring fork, but it used the same cable adjusting mechanism that had been used on other H-D Big Twins since 1928—a hollow bolt threads onto the brake coil, the coil and adjusting bolt are inserted through an unthreaded lug on the brake backing plate, and a nut locks them into adjustment. The backing plate also has a peened-on stud for the brake shackle. This backing plate is used for 1936–1937. The front drum was used from 1936 through 1939. The brake shackle has a grease fitting on each end, each pointing up. This shackle is correct for 1936–1938.

The 1936 61's rear brake drum and backing plate are one-year-only parts, used only on the OHV. The brake is 7 1/4 inches in diameter, the same as the front, and uses the same shoes as the front. About the only part of the assembly that was carried over to following years was the operating-cam lever, which was used on all the OHV rear brakes through 1957.

The pedal and linkage for the 1936 61's rear brake also had many one-year-only parts, including the pedal, pedal pivot, front operating rod, and the right-end lever for the crossover. The stamped-steel brake pedal has only three holes—the pivot hole at the bottom, a 5/16-inch upper hole into which the operating rod's end is inserted, and a 1/4-inch lower hole for the pedal return spring. (Pedals for 1937 and later had a fourth hole for the brake-lock lever's pivot bolt.) The pedal is cadmium plated.

The 1936-only operating rod has a 90-degree bend at each end; one end is inserted into a hole in the pedal, and the other end is inserted into a hole in the crossover shaft's right-end lever. The hooked ends were not ideal connections, however. Under hard braking, the ends would flex and bind, so the rod was replaced for 1937 by a rod with clevises at each end.

The basic front brake setup introduced in 1936 proved to be satisfactory, so it was carried over into the following years largely unchanged. By today's standards it would be called pathetic, but it was about as good as the brakes offered by the competition—and it was probably as powerful as the period tires could handle under normal road conditions. Anyway, riders of the day didn't know that front brakes offered far greater braking potential than rear brakes, for these were the days when the rear brake was considered to be the main brake by most motorcyclists. Thus, many riders who considered the front brake perfectly acceptable were less than satisfied with a rear brake of the same size. They had reason to be dissatisfied because the rear brake on the 61 was conspicuously weak and tended to chatter and squeal, so the 7-1/4-inch rear brake was used for 1936 only. In fact, many owners of 1936 61s upgraded to the larger rear brake when it became available in 1937, so the original 7-1/4-inch rear brake parts are scarce today.

Brown likes to restore his bikes and preserve them perfectly, seldom riding them but showing them at various meets so they can still be appreciated. Note the holes in the chrome plate atop the handlebar's center section. These appear only for 1936, and they are one of the many mysteries of the 1936 61. I have never heard a plausible answer for why the holes were drilled.

Continuing Problems

The 1936 Knucklehead was a basically sound design but a number of circumstances—H-D's understandable eagerness to recoup the new bike's high development costs, the cumulative financial squeeze of the Depression, labor laws that prevented H-D engineers from working overtime—combined to force H-D's management into ordering the new model shipped to dealers in a form that was essentially an advanced prototype. Predictable difficulties ensued, but the company rushed to correct these teething problems with updated parts and tuning information, sometimes modifying a single part three or more times during the production run. The daunting number of such changes made during the 1936 model year attests to the fact that its configuration had been far from finalized when the first bikes were shipped

The most chronic problem was the same one that is thought to have delayed the 61's introduction for so long—oil control. Even after the valve-spring covers were put into production, oil leaks were still prevalent. One of the main causes of leaks was improper adjustment of the oil supply to each rocker arm. A little well-intentioned tinkering could easily result in over- or under-oiled valves.

The consequences of over oiling were unpleasant but not catastrophic: excessive oil consumption and extreme leakage from the valve covers (they all leaked a bit anyway). Even so, it is easy to understand why a customer would be disappointed when his shiny new Knucklehead trailed a thick blue cloud of oil smoke, saturated his legs with oil, or consumed more lubricant than the previous Harleys with total-loss oil systems.

If the adjustment erred on the side of under-oiling, the consequences were much more serious, ranging from what *Shop Dope No. 140* described as "squeaking" valves, to rapid and excessive wear of the valves, rockers, shafts, and pushrods.

Even when valve oiling was properly adjusted, the valve spring covers sometimes overflowed with oil, because with each engine cycle the vacuum used to pull oil out of the covers

sucked debris into the cover to form a sludge that could plug the return lines. As a quick fix, an air fitting was added to the front rocker housing in late 1936, according to *Shop Dope No. 140A*, revised July 20, 1936. Pressurized air applied at the fitting unclogged both scavenge lines. The shop dope also gave instructions to add the air nipple to earlier engines. Of more catastrophic consequence, water could enter through the valve-arm slot, freezing the valve in a block of ice if the temperature dropped below freezing. These problems would not be fully fixed until 1938, when new covers

A photo of a 1936 police bike showing many of the features common to late-1936 machines: the "knuckle" nuts in place of the round chrome "frog-eye" covers over the ends of the rocker shafts, the air fitting on the front rocker housing, the one-piece front safety guard, and the unnotched gearcase cover. The speedometer is apparently equipped with a tripmeter, as inferred from the reset knob and rubber cover on the right side of the instrument panel. A look under the kickstarter return spring shows that even at the late date this machine was built, the adjustable support for the transmission was still in use. The fender pinstripes are worth noting in that a second pinstripe is painted along the junction of the black panel and white crown of the fenders, and the lower pinstripe on the front fender ends in a flourish at the rear. This photo also shows the "star" cover on the front hub, with a small 1936-only notch on each side of the axle. *Copyright Harley-Davidson Michigan, Inc.*

were introduced that fully enclosed each rocker arm and valve in its own housing.

The two-piece pinion-shaft assembly (through which oil passed to get to the crank pin and connecting-rod bearings) was also a cause of excessive oil consumption. Starting with engine number 36EL1755 (and 88 engines with lower serial numbers), a new stub shaft (the part of the pinion-shaft assembly that mounts to the flywheel) was fitted that reduced oil flow to the bottom end, according to *Shop Dope No. 142*. Harley-Davidson suggested that the new stub shaft be retrofitted in all earlier engines and made it available free of charge, on an exchange basis. The shop dope also reiterated that proper adjustment of oil to the rocker arms was critical to making the engine run well and get acceptable oil mileage.

Listed in the Shop Dope are the 88 earlier engines that were also fitted with the new stub shaft. Interestingly, the list includes *all* engines from 1722 to 1754, which makes me wonder, why didn't the Shop Dope say that the modification began with engine number 1722 instead of 1755? Also, the engines listed include six from the first 100 serial numbers

(including 1018, ostensibly the 18th engine built) and some from each subsequent 100. Why would all these very early engines still be at the factory when the engines with serial numbers over 1700 were being built? Had the earlier engines been returned for warranty work or had they remained at the factory for reworking of problems?

Competition

Even though the factory was unwilling to officially campaign the 61, private riders took up the mantle. As already mentioned, the Knucklehead was piloted to its first victory by "Butch" Quirk, who used a sidecar-equipped 61 to win a 350-mile endurance run sponsored by the Rose City Motorcycle Club. The March 23, 1936, dealer news bulletin announced that the 61 had been ruled eligible for Class C competition in the 80-ci class, and Knucklehead riders soon began competing and winning in numerous TTs, hillclimbs, and road races across the country. A rider even piloted a sidecar-equipped 61 to a gold medal in the grueling International Six-Day Trials, which were held in Germany that year. Though it wasn't a dominant racer in its first year, it would soon make its mark.

1936 Production

Just as the start date of 61 production is a mystery, so, too is the ending date and the number actually produced. As with the start date, I haven't found definitive answers for those questions. I have, however, gathered some information on these topics that I hope will add to the body of knowledge and spark further discussion on the issue.

Consensus among the many experts on the 1936 61 is that production began in March or April and ended in July. Information from dealer news bulletins suggests that both of these dates are suspect. As the dealer news bulletins quoted earlier in this chapter suggested, production probably began in early January and quickly ramped up. As winter turned to spring, orders began rolling in faster than they could be filled, as the February 24, 1936, dealer news bulletin had predicted.

The May 18 issue reassured dealers that "the 61 OHV delivery situation is getting better all the time!" and that production was "getting to a better stride." It went on to predict, "This is going to be welcome news indeed to our dealers who have been . . . fearful to give this model full selling justice because they were afraid of the delivery situation." It went on to state that orders could be filled in 8 to 10 days and also hinted at what a difficult task it had been to get the new model into production: "To us here at the scene it is nothing short of a miracle the way this factory has handled and brought on production of the new 61." Because the principles are all riding Harleys in the clouds, we'll never know what miracles were worked!

The immediate future. Demand grew for the 61 as the production year went on. The 1936 61s were built into at least late August 1936 (the August 10, 1936, dealer news bulletin specified that delivery time for 61s was "about two weeks"). The bike on the right, also owned and restored by Carman Brown, shows what the second-year Knuckleheads looked like.

As mentioned previously, the June issue of *The Enthusiast* contained an ad featuring the 61 OHV. The ad called the 61 the "Sensation of the motorcycle world," and accurately alluded to the conspicuous lack of promotion: "Minus fanfare and ballyhoo, a new motorcycle has come on the scene and has taken the world by storm." It also featured a photo of Bill Cummings, the winner of the 1934 Indianapolis 500, on his all-white (including frame, oil tank, and toolbox) 1936 61. This first official notice about the new model, in Harley's own magazine, came almost six months after the first 61s hit the streets.

The June 15 bulletin stated that orders could be filled in 7 to10 days if standard colors and equipment were ordered—more evidence that custom colors were available.

By the deadline for the August 10 issue, delivery time for 61s was up to "about two weeks." This is interesting not so much to show that orders were still coming in as strong at the end of summer as at the beginning, but because it implies that the 1936 61s were still in production in early August and that the final orders in at that time would not be filled until at least mid-August. The bikes discussed in the bulletin were almost certainly 1936 models, because the 1937 models were not announced to the dealers until the October 19 dealer news bulletin, and not to the public until the November issue of *The Enthusiast*.

From the information in these bulletins, a rough timeline can be drawn. Production of 61 demonstrators began no later than mid-January and finished sometime around the middle of February. Production of 61s to fill customer orders began in middle to late February and ended no sooner than mid-August.

So how many were built? Production figures compiled by Harley-Davidson and published in its book, *The Legend Begins*, suggest that 1,704 Knuckleheads were sold in 1936, including 152 Model Es, 1,526 Model ELs, and 26 Model ESs. Consensus among many experts (based on their observation of serial numbers of existing machines) is that closer to 2,000 were built, and this figure is supported by the November 1936 issue of *The Enthusiast*, which boasts that, "In the short time it has been out nearly 2,000 of these sweet jobs have been placed in owners' hand and are rolling up millions of economical miles on American highways." According to Jerry Hatfield, the company's board minutes said 61 sales totaled 1,836 through the end of the business year on September 30, 1936. The highest serial number I have heard of on an existing bike is 2903 (the 1,903rd built).

For some reason, the early machines seem to have survived in greater numbers than the later machines. Gerry Lyons, founder of the 36 EL Registry and editor of the club's newslet-ter, divided the serial numbers of the 1936 61s known to exist into two lists—those up to 2000 (e.g., the first 1,000 1936 61s built) and those over 2000. In theory, at least, survival rates should have been uniform across the serial-number range, resulting in a one-to-one ratio if 2,000 machines really were built. In fact, the ratio is two to one, in favor of the early bikes.

Why would almost twice the percentage of the early bikes survive? I can't think of an *obvious* reason for this to be the case, but there must be one, or else actual production was substantially less than 2,000. Several theories to explain the skewed ratio have been floated in the club's newsletter. Some theorize that whole blocks of late-serialed motorcycles may have been shipped overseas. Others theorize that Harley-Davidson skipped blocks of serial numbers to trick rival Indian into thinking the 61 was selling in greater numbers than was actually the case.

I find the first theory plausible. It is not inconceivable that Alfred Rich Child or another foreign franchisee would order 50 to 100 or more machines at once, all of which probably would have been built as a block, with consecutive serial numbers. According to the book *Harley-Davidson: The Milwaukee Marvel* by Harry Sucher, Child had exclusive sales rights for Japan, Korea, China, and Manchuria and could order machines on open account, with payment not due until 90 days after the shipment reached Japan. Sucher also says that Genijiro Fukui, a representative of Sankyo, "purchased several hundred sidecar outfits from [Child] in 1936" to "fill out their Rikuo line." Sankyo was by this time building the Rikuo, a license-built copy of the Harley-Davidson VL side-valve Big Twin, so it is unlikely that Sankyo would purchase side-valve sidecar rigs. It is quite possible that many of them were 61s. Similarly, other importers may also have bought large blocks of 61s, all or most of which were probably destroyed or ground up for scrap during World War II.

The second theory I find implausible. Why, when it had just released a motorcycle that set the lead in the big-twin market, and one it couldn't build fast enough to keep up with orders, would Harley-Davidson skip serial numbers just to fool the competition? I don't think they would.

Whatever the actual production figure was—1,704, 1,836, or 2,000—it exceeded Harley-Davidson's original sales projections. And demand exceeded the factory's production capacity. Clearly, the 61 was a hit. More important, the Knucklehead gave H-D a firm technological lead over arch rival Indian and their flat-head Chief. It also gave them an engine that was in the same technological league as the best European twins. Even though the Depression was far from over in the country at large, the future looked bullish from the boardroom in Milwaukee.

CHAPTER TWO

1937-1939

The Knucklehead Takes Over

T oday, we have a wonderful term that perfectly describes the reason for Harley-Davidson's reticent approach to publicizing the 1936 61: "plausible deniability." While the company hoped that the 61's unique combination of style and performance would bring success, it also knew the bike still had many flaws. Consequently, H-D did its best to keep the bike under wraps to ensure that if failure came, at least it would be a quiet one.

Fortunately, the 61 sold itself, and H-D did a superb job of fixing problems on the fly. Even so, some dealers and customers wondered whether they'd been used again as unpaid testers, a practice that is now common, especially in the software industry. And today, we have another term to describe less than fully developed products, such as the 1936 61, that are put onto the market for comment and debugging by favored customers: the "beta" release.

For 1937, H-D's efforts and its customers' patience were rewarded by the introduction of Knucklehead Version 1.0, a much-improved machine that was the product of lessons learned that first year. At the start of its second era, the Knucklehead began to take over. That year, all of the company's models were remade in its image, with revised, dry-sump motors clothed in 61-style finery. With full confidence in its OHV at last, H-D threw back the cloak of silence; the first year's lack of "fanfare and ballyhoo" gave way to a blizzard of promotion in the second, and sales of the 61 began a steady climb that accelerated in the following years. By the end of the decade, the 61 was poised to become Harley's best-selling motorcycle, even though it was also the company's most expensive.

Window to the World, 1937

By the start of the 1937 model year, most Americans believed that the worst days of the Depression were behind them, but the Depression was far from over. For 1937, unemployment and inflation were up slightly, and the Dow was down.

On January 20, FDR was inaugurated for his second term as president. His New Deal was given a big boost when conservative justice Willis Van DeVanter resigned and was replaced by Hugo L. Black. This swung the balance of the court to the left and promised an end to a string of New Deal acts that had been overturned by the Supreme Court.

On May 6, the German zeppelin *Hindenburg* was consumed by fire and crashed to Earth as it attempted to moor at Lakehurst, New Jersey, after a flight from Frankfurt-am-Main, Germany. More than 30 people were killed in the conflagration. Herbert Morrison's heart-wrenching eyewitness report of the tragedy was relayed around the country to become the first coast-to-coast radio broadcast.

On July 2, Amelia Earhart disappeared somewhere over the Pacific Ocean on her much-hyped attempt to fly around the world.

The 1939 models came closer to recapturing the sporty styling of the original Knuckleheads than did any other year. Note that the patent decal was moved back to the toolbox cover for 1939, where it had been in 1936. This stunning 1939 EL is owned and was restored by Eldon Brown. The solid Wolfe Safety wheels, made by Wolfe Accessory Mfg. Co., of Akron, Ohio, are period accessories that have been on the bike since it was new, according to Reg Shanks, the Vancouver Island, British Columbia, dealer who originally sold the bike in 1939.

New for 1937 was the 120-mile-per-hour speedometer with hash marks at the intermediate 5-mile-per-hour positions. It was available with or without a trip odometer. The trip-odometer version shown was used only for 1937. The version without the trip odometer was available through 1940. Also new for 1937 was the speedometer light switch, which is at the aft end of the skull-face dash.

On July 12, the U.S. Navy got a taste of things to come when the *USS Panay* was sunk by Japanese aircraft while in China's Yangtze River, killing two Americans. Two days later, Japan apologized and agreed to reparations.

In one of the more remarkable ironies of the era, amphetamines were introduced to "cure" hyperactive children in the same year that the Marijuana Taxation Act prohibited the importation, sale, or possession of the weed.

Labor unrest continued as nearly half a million workers participated in sit-down strikes. Industry responded with a heavy club. Labor organizer John L. Lewis uttered the most memorable mouthful of the year: "No tin-hat brigade of goose-stepping vigilantes or Bible-babbling mob of blackguarding corporation scoundrels will prevent the onward march of Labor." The song, *Whistle While You Work*, became a major hit.

The labor unrest was as strong in Milwaukee as it was elsewhere. In March, Harley-Davidson employees unionized under the United Auto Workers. On April 21, William A. Davidson, one of the four founders of the company, died. His son, William H. Davidson, was made a company vice president and was selected to eventually succeed Walter Davidson as president.

The 1937 Knucklehead

Harley's OHV Big Twin was offered in three versions for 1937: the high-compression 37EL Special Sport Solo, the medium-compression 37E Solo, and the medium-compression 37ES twin with sidecar gearing. All were listed at a retail price of $435.00. Essential equipment such as a jiffy stand and steering damper had to be ordered separately or as part of one of the option groups, at additional cost.

Two option groups for solos and one group for sidecar haulers were offered. The Standard Solo Group, which listed for $21.75, included the front safety guard, steering damper, ride control, stop light and switch, jiffy stand, trip odometer, and front fender light. The Deluxe Solo Group included all the items in the standard group plus a colored shift knob, footpedal rubbers, the Chrome Plate Group, a license-plate frame, the 6-inch round air cleaner, and the Deluxe Saddlebags. It listed for $49.00. The Standard Group for sidecar or commercial motorcycles, a $20.00 package, included a front safety guard, a steering damper, a stop light and switch, the ride control, and the three-speed transmission with reverse gear.

Styling Changes

The 1937 models came with a new paint scheme. The art deco gas-tank transfer was retained, but for 1937 the transfer was bracketed above and below by thick stripes edged in a complementary color. Gone were the 1936's fender panels, replaced by solid-color fenders with stripes matching those on the tank running along each side of each fender's crown. And the 1936 OHV's gorgeous color-matched rims were replaced in 1937 by black-painted rims.

Two regular civilian color combinations were listed in the November 1936 issue of *The Enthusiast*, which introduced the new-models for 1937: Bronze Brown striped in Delphine Blue and edged in yellow and Teak Red striped in black and edged in gold. The brown scheme proved to be unpopular, so a third combination was soon introduced: Delphine Blue striped in Teak Red. Police models were offered in Police Silver with black stripes edged in gold.

Of the three regular civilian combinations, the red and blue schemes proved to be the overwhelming preference of riders then and restorers now. Viewed from today's perspective on what is clearly an antique machine, the Bronze Brown and Delphine Blue is a handsome combination that seems suitable for the machine. But at the time, the brown paint projected a somewhat military or utilitarian image—not at all what most riders wanted on their expensive new sport machine—so it was never popular.

To compensate for the loss of color-matched wheel rims, the 1937 OHV was given a color-matched oil tank in place of the black tank of 1936, resulting in a motorcycle that "is one continuous sweep of color," according to the November 1936 issue of *The Enthusiast*. The new "sweep" of color might have been too much of a good thing, however. Color-matched oil tanks were discontinued at the end of 1937 and would not again be offered on the Harley-Davidson Big Twins until the special Hollywood Green paint package offered for the 1955 Panheads.

Engine Updates

Aside from the tendency to spit a bit of oil out of the minimal rocker covers, the new OHV mechanism introduced in and refined throughout 1936 proved to be remarkably

The frame for 1937 was much-improved over the 1936 frame, but it also was much heavier. The front downtubes are no longer continuous from a slash-cut single-butted joint below the steering head to the axle clips. Instead, stiffer straight tubes stretch from the steering head to the new sidecar-mount forgings. Separate tubes run back from the forgings to the axle clips. Many of the mounts were also made stronger to eliminate the chronic frame-cracking problems experienced with the 1936 Knucklehead frame. This frame also has the mount on the right lower frame tube for the kickstarter-side transmission mount that had been introduced on late-1936 frames. The transmission case was updated early in 1937 to have a cast-in boss to mount directly to the frame mount, eliminating the need for the separate bracket attached to the kickstarter cover that had been used in 1936. *Copyright Harley-Davidson Michigan, Inc.*

trouble-free. A weak point in the system was the somewhat willowy rocker-shaft support arms cast into the cylinder head. For 1936, the two support arms on each head had only a partial reinforcement rib that extended barely halfway up the arm, ending far below the level of the rocker-shaft holes. The problem with the design only came to light when the bikes were out on the street, being revved in friendly competition and fixed by owners and mechanics who had no experience with the new OHV system. During service work, these support arms are easily broken or over stressed if the shaft nuts are cinched up when everything is not correctly aligned or if the thrust washers are left out during assembly.

The solution? The support arms were increased in width, the reinforcing rib on each rocker-shaft support was lengthened, (now reaching vertically to the level of the rocker shaft,) and the ribs were cast integrally with the cooling fin to the left of the bracket. Other than this change to the support brackets, the heads were unchanged, retaining the cup-type valve-spring covers. This cylinder-head design is correct for 1937 only. They would be redesigned the following year to solve the other major problem with the OHV's cylinder

heads—oil leaking out and dirt and water leaking in through the valve enclosures.

Another chronic source of oil leaks was the cork rocker-arm seals in the aluminum rocker housings. Starting with serial number 37E1672, the cork seals were replaced by synthetic rubber seals. While these seals came into regular production on 37E1672, they were also fitted on 28 motors with earlier serial numbers that apparently had not been shipped yet for whatever reason, these serial numbers are listed in *Shop Dope No. 153*. That Shop Dope also instructed dealers to throw away any cork seals in stock and to only use the updated rubber seal on future repairs.

Just as in 1936, an air horn was standard on the OHV's carburetor, but the 1937 air horn was a new design. The new OHV air horn was a mirror image of the horn on the flathead Big Twins, a rounded, streamlined shape that tapers from front to rear. The 1937-style air horn was standard on OHVs through 1939.

Starting in 1937, an air cleaner was supplied as part of the Deluxe Solo Group, or it could be ordered separately for $3. This air cleaner is the 6-inch round air cleaner that had been optional for at least part of 1936. The cover is chrome-plated and has the Harley-Davidson bar-and-shield stamped into its round face and an instruction plate riveted to the rim. The cover is fastened to the backing plate by four screws. The oiled-copper-mesh air cleaner wraps around a mesh support welded to the steel backing plate. The backing plate is Parkerized.

The ignition timer was also slightly revised for 1937. The new timer base is like the previous base, except that the notch in the side of the base for the circuit-breaker wire is omitted, and the wire attaches to a terminal post below the base. The wire is routed out of the timer through a hole added to the revised timer housing. This new timer base and housing were used through the end of the Knucklehead line in 1947.

About midway through the 1937 production run, the rocker arms were revised to include an oil passage to positively lubricate the pushrod ball socket. Prior to this modification, the pushrod-to-pushrod-ball bearing surface was oiled only by scavenged oil pulled from the valve-spring covers by engine vacuum. If the return oil lines from the valve-spring covers were plugged or if the oil supply to the valves was adjusted down for minimal overspray, the pushrods would be under-oiled and would wear prematurely. These revised rocker arms were used for the remainder of the 1937 production and through early-1939 production.

Frame and Fifth Transmission Mount

Like the rest of the 1936 OHV, that bike's double-down-tube frame was a radical departure for a Harley-Davidson street bike. And like the rest of the bike, the frame needed a good bit of tweaking to get it right. Hard use on street and track, and especially under heavy-duty police and sidecar duty, quickly proved that the original design wasn't stout enough for the job. The frame tended to crack under the seat post and at the transmission mount, and the left rear stay sometimes snapped off behind the clutch, so a substantially

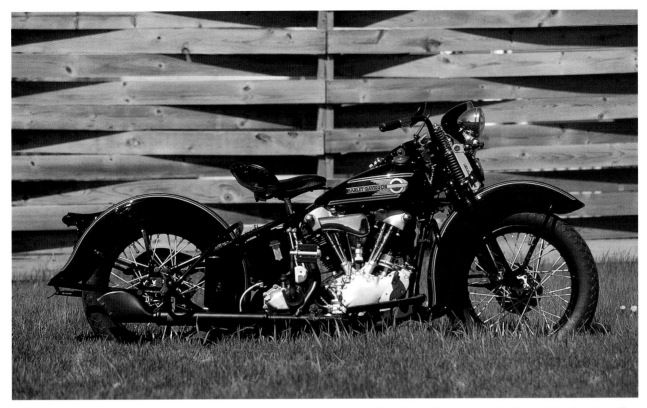

The streamlined air horn shown replaced the slash-cut air horn used in 1936. Elmer Ehnes restored this machine for himself, but he does some of the nicest Knuckle and Panhead restorations out of his home shop and that of Kokesh Motorcycles in Spring Lake Park, Minnesota.

redesigned frame made its appearance for the second year of 61 OHV production.

Gone were the two continuous downtubes that swept down and back from the steering head to the axle clips. Replacing them were larger diameter tubes that make the same sweep, but each is formed in two sections. The first section on each side connects the steering head to the top of a new drop forging that has integral sidecar mounting loops. The second section connects to the bottom of the sidecar-mount forging and sweeps down and back to the axle clips. The new frame is stiffer in torsion, improving handling, and it proved much more resistant to cracking than the 1936 frame had been.

The sidecar-mount forgings replace the sidecar loops that were brazed or welded onto the continuous downtubes in 1936. The new mounts strengthen the frame and provide a much more durable mounting location for the sidecar.

The 1937 and later frames were also fitted with the brazed-on clamp bracket for the starter-end, "fifth" transmission mount that had been fitted to a few of the last 1936 frames.

To further strengthen the attachment of the transmission to the frame, the transmission mounts were made stronger, and the transmission mounting plate was twice as thick as that used in 1936. All these modifications helped tremendously, but the problem wasn't really fixed until midyear, when a new transmission case was introduced that had a starter-support boss designed into the casting, which replaced the support

bracket bolted to the kickstarter cover. This new transmission case was not replaced until the 1940 model year.

Transmission and Clutch Updates

At about the same time as the transmission case was revised, the starter cover was also modified. The new cover looks, externally, like the previous cover, but is substantially revised internally. The machined-in area for the cork seal on the old cover was replaced with a slight recess for the starter-crank washer. The seal was no longer needed because the one-piece crank bushing used with the old cover was replaced by a two-piece bushing with a neoprene seal between the inner and outer length of bushing. Also, the reinforcing ribs around the starter-shaft tunnel were made thicker and a fifth rib was added.

The new cover continued in production through midyear 1938. This new cover and bushing, in concert with the fifth transmission mount, made the whole starter system stout enough to withstand the vigorous kicking sometimes required to start the OHV.

But it wasn't just the transmission mounts and frame that were prone to breakage under severe use. On rare occasion, the transmission mainshaft would crack at its clutch-hub end, so about midway through the production run, a revised transmission mainshaft and mainshaft nut were phased in. The new mainshaft differed from the old only in that the clutch-hub end of the shaft was increased to 3/4 inch in diameter (it

A 1937 EL restored and owned by Carman Brown. The fender stripes shown replaced the fender panels used in 1936. Standard wheel rims for 1937 were painted black, but cadmium-plated rims were available for 50 cents each, or bolt-on chrome wheel rings were available for $5. Note that the rear mount for the chain guard is now part of the fender-stay clip, unlike the 1936-only separate bracket that was riveted to the fender stay.

had been 11/16 inch), and the nut was increased in inside diameter to fit the new shaft. These revisions apparently fixed the problem because the mainshaft and nut were not revised again until mid-1950, when it was being used on the Knucklehead's successor, the Panhead.

The Knucklehead's clutch also suffered under severe use, especially under the incessant stop-and-go use motorcycles were subjected to in traffic-control or escort service with police departments. Under such use, the driving disc heated up from friction with the outermost fiber disc and conducted the heat to the clutch springs, ruining their temper.

To solve the problem, Harley-Davidson engineers revised the clutch pack that was incorporated into new machines starting after May 1, according to *Shop Dope No. 166*. The outer fiber disc was replaced by a steel sprung disc of a new design, and the original "humped" sprung disc was replaced by a plain steel disc. The new sprung disc has eight long, thin, L-shaped slots cut into its outer circumference and notches on its inner circumference to mate with the splines on the driving disc. This disc pack has one fewer fiber disc, one more steel disc,

and a redesigned sprung disc. Unfortunately, the revisions to the clutch pack didn't really solve the problem, so the clutch would be redesigned again in mid-1938.

New, Larger Rear Brake

The 1936 61's brakes, however anemic by today's standards, were as good as most of the day. But they still had some shortcomings, especially the rear brake. Though the 1936 rear brake is the same size as the front brake (7 1/4-inch drum inside diameter), and in theory just as powerful, it was considered too to be too weak. The standard way to make brakes more powerful was to increase their size. So for 1937 Harley-Davidson introduced a new rear brake with an 8-inch inside diameter, larger and more powerful than the front brake.

While this bias toward rear brake power on a sport bike may seem odd in light of today's sport bikes with huge, full-floating twin front discs and much smaller rear discs, it was not unusual in the 1930s. Back then, the rear brake was still considered by most riders to be the primary brake, and the larger brake would remain in the rear through the end of Knucklehead production in 1947.

The 8-inch rear brake assembly fitted to the 1937 models was all new, from the drum and backing plate to the shoes. The new rear-brake backing plate was stamped steel, with a six-pointed star pattern around the axle hole. Its anchor tab on the plate's outside surface is reinforced by a plate that wraps about 1/3 of the way around the flat part of the backing plate and is attached with nine rivets to the inside surface of the backing plate. This backing plate was painted black and was used for 1937 only.

The rear brake drum was also stamped steel. Its swept surface is 8 inches in diameter for a substantial increase in braking surface over the previous rear drum. As before, the brake drum featured five dowel pins and five holes for the screws to attach the drum to the wheel hub. With this increase in power, the Knucklehead's rear drum had reached its final form, being used until the line was replaced by the Panhead series for 1948. Rear drums were painted black.

In addition to increasing the diameter of the drum, Harley-Davidson engineers gave the new brake shoes longer linings. Unlike the shoes on the 1936 brake, the shoes on the 1937 brake are not interchangeable. These shoes have a-1 11/64-inch-wide pivot end for the early-style pivot stud and use a return spring for each shoe. These shoes and spring were used through early-1938 production.

The pedal and linkage for the rear brake were also updated for 1937. The brake rod was redesigned to substitute stout clevis connections for the 90-degree bends used in 1936. The 1937 rod was given a shallow S bend to allow for the horizontal offset between the foot pedal and the crossover lever, and the rod was threaded at each end for the clevises. This new rod remained in use through 1947. The rod's front clevis is 2 7/16 inches long; its rear clevis is 1-7/8 inches long. The longer front clevis was used for 1937 and 1938, but the 1 7/8-inch rear clevis was used through 1947. Brake rods and clevises were Parkerized.

The brake pedal and crossover-shaft lever were subtly revised for use with the new clevises. Like the 1936 pedal, the

Brown's 1937 EL wears what Harley-Davidson hoped would be their signature paint combination for 1937—Bronze Brown with Delphine Blue striping edged in gold. To popularize their new models, they printed up a two-color brochure printed in the new color and touting the beautiful appearance it gave to the 1937 machines.

early 1937 pedal has only two holes (for the operating rod and the brake return spring) near the large pivot hole. For 1937, the operating-rod hole was reduced from 5/16 inch to 1/4 inch for the clevis pin. The crossover-shaft lever's brake-rod hole was also reduced in diameter to 1/4 inch, and another hole was added to the lever for attachment of the sidecar brake rod. The brake pedal is cadmium plated on early machines but was Parkerized on later machines.

According to *The Enthusiast* of November 1936, the new brakes and linkage prevented "bending and bucking" and loss of power. "You get real braking action and you can 'whoa' your iron hoss down in a hurry," boasted the magazine.

More changes were made to the rear brakes as model year 1937 progressed because some rear brake units were prone to chattering and "self-energizing" under severe braking.

The main cause of these problems was thought to be excessive clearance between the brake's operating shaft and the shaft's nonreplaceable steel bearing sleeve, and the problem only got worse as time and use increased clearance further. If the chattering became severe enough, "[t]he shock wave . . . sometimes breaks off brake cover torque stud or lug which allows the cover to turn, and breakage of operating shaft follows putting brake completely out of commission," according to *Shop Dope No. 157*. To help solve the problem, a replaceable bronze bushing that was finished-reamed to a closer tolerance was added to the operating shaft hole in the rear backing plate starting on January 11, 1937. The new bushing could also be fitted to earlier machines if the backing plate was reamed for the new bushing.

The new bushing and tighter clearances went a long way toward curing the chattering problem but did not reduce the brake tendency to "self-energize," or grab and lock. On April 13, 1937, *Shop Dope No. 157-A* was released that suggested that the solution to the problem lay in grinding back the brake linings 5/8 inch from the pivot-stud end and 1 3/4 inches from the operating cam end on those brakes that self-energized. The shorter linings were able to bear more evenly on the drum and greatly reduced brake squeal and sudden lock-up.

Late in 1937, a new, optional rear parking brake lock was offered, and the foot pedal was drilled with an additional hole, about halfway up the lever, for the pivot bolt of the parking brake lock's saw-toothed lever.

Several updates for 1937 are featured in this photo. Underneath the footboard is the improved brake rod with clevises at each end. Holes on both the brake pedal and crossover lever were reduced in diameter from 5/16 inch to 1/4 inch for the clevis pins. Early in the year, the brake pedal was cadmium-plated, as shown, but later pedals were Parkerized. For 1937, the main oil feed line to the oil pump connects to a fitting on the bottom of the tank at the drain hole, rather than at a separate fitting at the back of the tank. While the new fitting configuration may have simplified construction of the oil tank, it made oil changes messier, so it was used for 1937 only. Oil tanks were painted the main color of the bike for 1937 (instead of being painted black) and had a patent decal on each side of the tank. Note the air nipple on the front rocker housing. This feature had been added in late 1936 and was used again in 1937 because the 1937 models were fitted with the same cup-type valve-spring enclosures that had been used in 1936. The return lines from the enclosures were prone to clogging, resulting in the covers filling with oil and spilling it all over the machine and rider—hence the tall boots worn by this rider. Air pressure applied at the nipple would (if the rider was lucky) clear all four return lines at once. *Copyright Harley-Davidson Michigan, Inc.*

New Oil-Tank Feed-Line Connection

For 1937 only, the oil tank's feed-line attached to a special connection on the tank's drain opening underneath the right side of the tank, rather than at its former position on the back of the tank's right side. The new drain plug is really a valve with a banjo fitting on its side for attachment of the feed line and a special internal valve that prevents the oil from draining when the feed line is disconnected.

The 1937 oil tank is like the late-1936 tank, with the embossed top and swaged-in banjo fittings, but the feed-line fitting at the back is omitted on the new tank. And, as previously mentioned, the tank was painted the same color as the gas tanks and fenders. In addition, patent decals were applied to both sides of the tank.

In use, the new valve and feed-line configuration proved troublesome and leak-prone and made maintenance more difficult, so it was used only for 1937. The 1938-and-later models were again fitted with oil tanks having the feed connection on the right back of the tank.

A screen was fitted from top to bottom inside the oil tank to filter out large particles of debris before they reached the feed line to the oil pump. In cold weather, frost from condensation in the oil sometimes partially or wholly clogged this screen, keeping the cold-thickened oil from reaching the feed fitting and starving the oil pump. Harley-Davidson fixed the problem on new machines starting on January 20, 1937, by cutting out the screens on tanks so fitted and omitting the screens on subsequent tanks. *Shop Dope No. 159* recommended that owners of earlier machines who rode their machines in subfreezing weather cut out the screen with a screwdriver or chisel. For riders who rode in consistent temperatures of 15 to 20 degrees or colder, *Shop Dope* recommended adding up to 1 3/4 pints of kerosene to H.D.'s medium-heavy oil to keep it from congealing. It gave no advice on how to keep the rider's blood from congealing.

Speedo Light Switch and
120-Mile-Per-Hour Speedometer

The tank-mounted instrument console and speedo-meter introduced in 1936 became instant classics, so Harley-Davidson wisely made only minor revisions to them for 1937. The instrument-panel cover benefited from the addition of a hole just rearward of the ignition switch for the newly added speedometer-light switch. This new switch allowed the rider to turn off the speedometer light independently of the main headlight switch. The new switch's knob is tube shaped, with a ball on each end, kind of like a barbell. The tubular portion is

knurled, and the whole knob is cadmium plated. This style of knob was used only for 1937 and 1938.

All 1937 instrument-panel covers had a hole on the right side for the trip odometer reset shaft, whether or not the motorcycle was fitted with a tripmeter-equipped speedometer. The hole for the reset was sealed with a rubber grommet that had an opening for the reset rod if one was fitted.

In a somewhat optimistic move, but one in keeping with the sporting image of the machine, a new, 120-mile-per-hour face was added to tripmeter and nontripmeter speedometers for 1937. The styling of these speedometers is like the styling of the 100-mile-per-hour speedometer of 1936, except that the numerals 110 and 120 were added. A speedometer without a tripmeter was standard, but a speedometer with tripmeter was fitted if either of the two option groups were ordered, or it could be ordered in place of the standard speedometer for $3. The 120-mile-per-hour speedometer with 5-mile-per-hour hashmarks and a tripmeter was used only for 1937, but the same speedo without a tripmeter was used from 1937 through 1940.

New Tankshift Lever and Gate

The 1936 OHV's shift lever, with its spring-loaded-plunger detent mechanism, was elegant. After disengaging the clutch by rocking the clutch foot pedal back, the rider would just push the shift lever forward or pull it back to change gears. The action was smooth, and shifts could be made more rapidly than on any other hand-shifter of the period. But over time and after many shifts, the plunger and its mating recess in the tank-mounted shifter gate sometimes wore to the point that the tankshift lever could skip or be bumped past its detent, possibly nudging the transmission out of gear under certain conditions. Truth be known, this shifter system was probably too elegant to be practical on a hard-ridden street machine. It was also expensive to produce and assemble, so Harley-Davidson engineers simplified the tankshift assembly with the introduction of a new tankshift lever and shifter gate for 1937.

The new tankshift lever was oval in section, making it more streamlined and stiffer for less fore and aft flex than was the tubular lever it replaced. The new lever was held firmly in each gear position by an individual detent notch in the new shifter gate.

The shifter mechanism on the transmission received a new shift gear on the shift cam for 1937. The new gear has teeth only one-third of the way around its circumference. The new shift gear was used from 1937 to 1947.

Miscellaneous Changes

The narrow, unreinforced fender tabs on the 1936 front forks were prone to cracking, so a plate was spot-welded on the underside of each tab for 1937. While this helped delay the onset of cracking, it didn't entirely cure the problem. As a result, the fender tabs were redesigned for the following year; the fork with narrow, reinforced tabs is a 1937-only part. Also, the fork's top plate was updated for 1937 to omit the four small holes that it had for at least part of 1936.

For 1937, the rear fender's left brace clip was fitted with a slotted, hook-shaped tab that served as the rear mounting point for the rear chainguard. This new tab replaced the separate mounting bracket that was riveted to the rear fender's frontmost brace on the left side on 1936 Knuckleheads.

Like the brake pedal, the clutch pedal was cadmium plated for at least part of the 1937 production year. Later pedals were Parkerized. The chrome-plated chain-inspection cover was standard for 1936 and 1937 also. Starting in 1938, it was painted black.

Square slots near the center hole of the star-shaped hub cover were omitted on all 1937 models. (These holes were part of the speedometer-drive mechanism on the 45-ci solo models for 1935–1936.) This revised star cover was used through the end of Knucklehead production in 1947. It was cadmium plated through about midyear and Parkerized thereafter.

Redesigned spokes were introduced to reduce problems with stretching and breakage under severe use, according to *Shop Dope No. 162*. The new spokes had a shorter head end (7/32 inch versus 11/32 inch) that was bent at a 105-degree angle (rather than a 90-degree angle). The shop dope specified that only the new-type spokes be used on all future service work and that any old-style spokes be returned for exchange on new-style spokes.

Finally, a terminal post was added to the seat-post mast to provide for a short wire to the battery, and oil-soaked felt washers were fitted to each battery post to retard corrosion.

RIGHT: Note the way the chain pull for the brake-light switch attaches to the brake rod. Also note the swaged fittings on the oil tank. These fittings had been introduced in late 1936, changed from welded-on fittings. Nineteen thirty-seven was the last year for the oil sending line (the cloth-covered line stretching up and back from the oil pump) from the oil pump to the mechanical oil-pressure indicator on the instrument panel.

Competition

In its second year, the 61 OHV began to make its way into the winner's circle and into the record books. On March 13, Joe Petrali piloted a specially prepared 61 to a new AMA straightaway record of 136.183 miles per hour. On April 8, a true iron-man named Fred Ham took a day off from his job as a motorcycle cop to try to break the world record for the number of miles ridden in 24 hours. He used a stock 61 that he had purchased in October 1936, and he planned to do all the riding himself. With the help of a crew of over 20, oil flares to mark the course at night, and quarts of cold milk to keep him alert, Ham rode 1,825 miles, an average of 76.6 miles per hour, for the record (he also broke 44 other intermediate records). On May 16, Al Aunapa rode his 61 to victory in the 100-mile TT National Championship.

1937 Production

The 61 OHV found even wider acceptance in its second year, as did the flathead 45s and Big Twins that were given the OHV's styling for 1937. Overall, Harley-Davidson's sales rose by a satisfying 19 percent. Of the 11,674 Harleys built that year, 2,205 were 61s. This total includes 126 E, 1,829 EL, and 70 ES. The following year would bring further improvement to the Knucklehead, curing at last the problem that had contributed so much to its delayed introduction and had given owners of 1936 and 1937 Knuckleheads such fits: oil leaks from the valve gear.

Window to the World, 1938

The U.S. economy was in a recession within a depression for most of 1938. In an attempt to pull the economy out of its extra-deep doldrums, Congress passed the Revenue Bill of 1938, an early version of supply-side economics that centered around corporate tax relief.

Americans had even bigger problems emerging overseas. In Europe, the Fascists were on the march. German forces "annexed" Austria. Not satisfied, Hitler then pressed for a takeover of the Sudetenland, which was then part of Czechoslovakia. In September, Britain and France agreed to give it to him. British Prime Minister Neville Chamberlain predicted "peace in our time." But Winston Churchill foresaw what was to come and rose to prominence, decrying Chamberlain's "appeasement" of Germany.

FDR wasn't fooled, either. He requested and received more than $1 billion in additional military spending.

In the United States, labor unrest continued, but subsided to a whimper after passage of the Wages and Hours Act,

Record-Breaking Knucklehead

O nce sales success of the 61 was certain, the company decided to build a special Knucklehead to go after the AMA straightaway record, with Joe Petrali as rider. The bike they built was almost completely custom-built for the record attempt, with a twin-carb engine, lightened frame, and shrouds and tailpiece with classic 1930s streamlined styling.

Interestingly, the engine in the restored machine is not the one shown in photos taken at the time. That engine, 37EL1002, is missing, and was replaced by the present engine, with the nonsensical engine number 36EL9991001, sometime after the record runs. Several engines were likely built, and the present engine may have been pieced together from spare parts because it is not complete, lacking pistons, connecting rods, and flywheels. Still it does have many of the special parts made just for the record-attempt bike. Its stroke was about 3/4-inch shorter than stock, so shortened barrels were fitted. Shortened pushrod retainers allowed the pushrods covers to telescope inward to accommodate the stroke.

Each head has a cast-in manifold on the left side for its own carburetor. The end of each manifold was drilled with a pattern of five holes to accommodate a two- or three-bolt carburetor. The carburetors fitted to this engine are Linkert MR-2 "barrel" racing carburetors—each had a revolving barrel rather than a butterfly valve in the throat—that fed special racing fuel to the engine. A magneto mounted in place of the generator supplied the ignition. Exhaust pipes were bobbed, ending just below the lower frame rails.

To save weight, the primary chain was replaced by a single-row 520 chain that transferred engine power to a VL clutch, which was engaged or released by a cut-off foot lever in nearly the same location as on a stock machine. Instead of a transmission, a special "in-or-out" single-ratio gear box was fitted. The box could be shifted in or out of gear, but the lever was not accessible to the rider; five pieces of shrouding had to be removed to access the lever. A VL kicker cover was fitted to the right end of the box, but the kickstart lever was omitted. Curiously, the hole for the lever's shaft was plugged by a wine cork. According to accounts of the record run, the bike was towed up to speed by another vehicle, then Petrali engaged the clutch to start the engine.

The frame had double downtubes, but it had no seat post, and the rear of the axle clips were bobbed to allow quick tire changes. Special rearset brackets were added to the frame for the bicycle-style pedals that served as foot pegs. Standard Knucklehead gas tanks were mounted on the frame. Curiously, the gas tanks and the handlebar fairing were chrome plated before painting.

In another effort to save weight, the Knucklehead forks and front wheel were exchanged for the slimmer and lighter pieces off a 1915 H-D.

Although H-D's efforts at streamlining ultimately proved counter productive, the shrouds dominated the look of the machine. Streamlining the front end were a small fairing and shrouds over the fork legs. The fairing was formed of a Knucklehead gas tank that had been cut and reshaped. In addition, the front wheel was also shrouded, giving it the look of a disc wheel. Wheel spokes were wired where they crossed with six wraps of wire, which were then soldered in place. The streamlining was completed by a boattail tailpiece that extended under the crankcase. (When the bike was disassembled for restoration, the extension had a layer of what appeared to be real Daytona sand). Shrouds and tailpiece were made of aluminum, but the joints between pieces were often leaded, which would seem to cancel out any weight savings. A seat built into the tailpiece placed Petrali much farther back than the normal riding position so he could bend forward, resting his chest against a pad on the gas tanks, arms stretching forward to the downwardly bent bars. Recesses for Petrali's legs were designed into the tailpiece and are similar to those later used on the original Harley-powered Buell motorcycles.

From his crouched position, Petrali had a good view of the handlebar-mounted tachometer, the bike's lone instrument. The tachometer was made from a stock speedometer by laying a hand-painted face over the speedo's face. A drive cable for the tachometer was spliced into the right crankcase's ignition-timer hole. The tach read from 2,000 to 7,000 rpm, with a 5,500-rpm redline.

Petrali made his first record-run attempts on March 12, 1937, on Daytona Beach. On the first day, heavy winds slowed him on the northbound leg of his runs, and spray from the surf sometimes wet the

On March 13, 1937, Joe Petrali rode this specially built Knucklehead to a new AMA straightaway record of 136.183 miles per hour on the sand at Daytona Beach. His efforts to break the record the day before had been foiled by ocean spray, heavy winds, and instability caused by some of the bike's streamlined bodywork. The tailpiece was removed for the record runs on the 13th. *Copyright Harley-Davidson Michigan, Inc.*

spark plugs and caused misfiring on the southbound leg. Worse, Petrali was forced to back off the throttle on the last northbound leg because the bike's front wheel was lifting off the sand. The record attempt was postponed until the next day. That night, the tailpiece and wheel covers were removed.

The wind eased somewhat by the time Petrali started his first run on the 13th. This run, too, was spoiled by ocean spray. The next run gave Petrali the new record, with an average speed of 134.83 miles per hour, beating the old record by just 2.81 miles per hour. The 61 was parked, and Petrali climbed aboard a 45 to set a new speed record for that class.

Even though he had already set two records that day, Petrali was not yet through. He climbed aboard the 61 again for another run. When the V-twin roared to life, he rocketed away from the pull-start vehicle on his way to a run with a two-way average of 136.183 miles per hour, beating his own record by about 1.5 miles per hour.

The bike Petrali rode was recently restored by Harley's on-staff restoration expert, Ray Schlee, and is part of H-D's traveling display. If anyone out there knows where the record-breaker's engine is, the factory has made it known that they'd like to buy it and bring it home.

The most obvious change for 1938 was the new striping on the tank. Rather than stripes above and below the tank transfers, the 1938 machines had a single stripe on each tank, extending forward and back from the tank transfers. This 1938 EL is owned by the enigmatic "Farmer Fred." Although it has a lot of extra chrome and nonstandard parts, it illustrates well the style of the 1938 Knuckleheads.

which raised the minimum wage to 40 cents per hour and limited weekly hours to 44.

Aviation was in the news. On July 14, Howard Hughes completed an around-the-world flight in 3 days, 19 hours, and 14 minutes. On July 17, Douglas "Wrong Way" Corrigan became a national celebrity when he took off for California, but landed in Dublin, Ireland. The part he left out of his story was that he had been denied a permit to fly to Europe.

On a visit to Milwaukee some time after his wrong-way flight, Corrigan asked for a ride on the machine of his dreams, a 1938 EL. After trading a limousine for 38EL3325 at the city limits, Corrigan raced south for the airport, leaving his entourage and police escort far behind. When the speedy flier reached the airport, he was heard to exclaim, "There is a real motorcycle!" Others raced their 61s to good effect that year, too. Sixty-ones carried their riders to victory in the 80-ci Pacific Coast TT Championship, the Southwestern TT Championship, and the Jack Pine Endurance Run.

The 1938 Knucklehead

As the October 1937 issue of *The Enthusiast* pointed out, the changes for 1938 were an "inside story" and one whose main theme was "smoother, quieter, cleaner." And, as we shall see, these were apt descriptions of the updated model.

The OHV Big Twin model line was paired down to just two offerings for 1938: the high-compression 38EL Special Sport Solo and the medium-compression 38ES twin with sidecar gearing. Accordingly, all nonpolice solo models should be marked 38EL and all nonpolice bikes marked 38E (remember, the S in ES was not marked on the crankcase as part of the serial number) should be sidecar or commercial machines. Most police solo models were probably 38Es, however, and some civilian solo 38Es were probably special ordered, so solo-models marked 38E undoubtedly were built.

Both the EL and ES were fitted with the high-domed, high-compression pistons for 1938 because the low-domed, medium-compression pistons had been discontinued at the end of the 1937 model year. The ES was given a lower compression ratio by fitting a compression plate underneath each cylinder. Gearing for the two models was unchanged.

All models were listed at a retail price of $435 (the same price as in 1937) but, for the first time, had to be ordered with one of the option groups, at additional cost.

Two option groups for solos and one group for sidecar haulers were offered. The Standard Solo Group included the front safety guard, steering damper, stop light and switch, jiffy stand, trip odometer, and front fender light and listed for $16.70 (which was about $5.00 cheaper than in 1937, probably because the ride control was no longer part of the package). The $49.75 Deluxe Solo Group included all the items in the standard group plus four-ply tires, ride control, a colored shift knob, the 6-inch round air cleaner, the Deluxe Saddlebags, and the Chrome Plate Special (includes chrome-plated handlebars, headlamp, instrument panel, wheel rings, parking lights, fender strips, and license-plate frame). The Standard Group for sidecar or commercial motorcycles, a $14.25 package, included a front safety guard, a steering damper, a stop light and switch, and ride control. (Note that the three-speed transmission with reverse gear was no longer part of the package.)

Color Harmony

The standard paint scheme was revised for the new model year. Once again, the art deco gas-tank transfer was retained and the gas tanks and fenders are painted in a solid color without panels, but for 1938 a thin stripe outlined in a complementary color runs down the centerline of the tank sides and aft of the tank transfer. A similar stripe curves along the top of the fender skirt, much farther down the sides of the fenders than the stripes used the previous year. And the oil tank is painted black for 1938, reversing the change to a color-matched tank that had been made for 1937.

Standard 1938 paint colors were Teak Red with black stripes edged in gold, Venetian Blue with white stripes edged in Burnt Orange, Hollywood Green with gold stripes edged in black, and Silver Tan with Sunshine Blue stripes. Police models were painted silver with black stripes.

Color harmony was the stated goal of some plating changes for 1938. "Chrome parts which only dazzled and did not carry out the color harmony of the machine were eliminated," according to an ad in the October 1937 issue of *The Motorcyclist*. The ad went on to specify that the timer cover was now plated in cadmium rather than chrome and that the "chain inspection cover on all models is now black and adds to the color harmony of the lower part of the machine." Most cadmium plating was also eliminated. According to the ad, "as soon as possible all nuts and bolts will be Parkerized instead of cadmium plated."

Fully Enclosed Rockers and Valves

Even when the adjustable rocker-oiling system was properly adjusted on the 1936 and 1937 machines, a fine mist of oil was continually vented out the rocker-arm opening in the valve-spring enclosures. It was nothing serious, but irritating nonetheless. As an ad in the October 1937 issue of *The Motorcyclist* admitted, "Oil seepage resulting in dirty motors and making for soiled clothing has been an evil that has been the source of much complaint in the past. With the growing popularity of light-colored riding clothing, especially club uniforms, the need for clean motors is self-evident."

Of greater import, if oil spray could leak out, dirt and water could leak in, quickly ruining valves and guides—not to mention the rockers and shafts, which were almost completely exposed to the elements. Worse yet, the dirt did not just leak in; it was actually sucked in by the engine vacuum used to scavenge oil from the valve-spring enclosure. And this dirt was then ingested into the engine along with the scavenged oil.

After two full years of complaints and warranty repairs, Harley-Davidson chose to fix the problem once and for all, by introducing truly effective full enclosures for the rocker arms and valves for 1938. One of these new enclosure assemblies was used for each valve, and each assembly consisted of a lower cover, a cover cap, a gasket, two screw plates, and screws.

The lower cover was a curiously shaped stamping with a lower cup that enclosed the valve stem and spring. An oil-scavenge line was attached to the right side of the cup, and a "trough" extended to the right to hold the rocker seal in place and cover the lower half of the rocker and shaft. A flange on the valve guide fastened the lower cover to the cylinder head, and an asbestos gasket was sandwiched between the cover and the cylinder head.

A separate cap completed the valve enclosure, covering the top of the pocket and the trough. The cap-to-cover junction was sealed by a gasket, then fastened together by screws that were inserted through holes in the cap, gasket, and lower cover and tightly cinched into threaded holes in two separate screw plates for each enclosure.

The oil lines from the lower cover were larger in diameter than the lines used the previous year (to reduce the tendency for them to clog) and attached to larger-diameter fittings on the rocker boss. A small vent hole allowed air to enter the enclosure when engine vacuum scavenged oil from the lower cover. Its location on the lower cover prevented water from dripping in, and its small size kept dirt ingestion to an acceptable minimum.

The new enclosures were a welcome improvement over the old type. Oil consumption decreased, and the bike stayed cleaner, inside and out. They worked so well that the enclosure stampings remained unchanged through 1947. (The screws and screw plates were updated in 1939, however.) Rocker enclosures were painted black.

Harley-Davidson even offered a kit to retrofit the new enclosures to 1936–1937 cylinder heads, and most of the older machines that exist today have these enclosures. *Shop Dope No. 172* gave instructions for the retrofit, and even mentioned that the factory would perform the work if the heads were returned to Milwaukee.

Cylinder-head cooling fins were relieved to allow clearance for the enclosures, but the castings were otherwise unchanged on early- through mid-1938 machines. Later in the 1938 production run, the cylinder head castings were again modified, this time to further stiffen the rocker-arm supports on the left side of the castings and provide more clearance for the rocker covers. The revised supports still joined in the center to form a V, but the V now had a flat atop each branch of the V, running from the reinforcing rib on the inside of the V to its rounded outside tip. The rocker-shaft

For 1938, the fender stripes were moved down to the top edge of the valance. Chrome-plated rims, hubs, and forks are not standard.

holes were no longer on the centerline of each ear of the V; rather, they were to the outside of the centerline, centered on the radius of the outer rounded tip. Head castings with the new rocker supports and drilled primer-cup bosses were used only on later-1938 machines.

Because the new rocker enclosures also held the rocker-arm seal in place in the aluminum rocker housing, the snap ring that held the seal in place on 1936–1937 motors was no longer needed. Consequently, both the front and rear rocker housings were revised to omit the groove that held the snap ring in place. The new rocker covers were so efficient at keeping out dirt and water that the oil-scavenge lines from the covers were no longer prone to clogging up with oil-dirt-water sludge, so the new front-head rocker housing was further revised to omit the air nipple that had been added in mid-1936. The rear head's rocker housing was fitted with an adapter for its exhaust valve's rocker enclosure. Rocker housings with these revisions were used through mid-1939.

The final top-end update for 1938 was to the exhaust valve's lower spring collar. The 1936 through early-1938 collar with an inside diameter of 21/32 inch was replaced in mid-1938 by the same lower spring collar (with an inside diameter of 27/32 inch) used on the intake valve.

Only a minor update was made to the engine's lower end, and it, too, continued the themes of "smoother, quieter." In a move to make their timing gears more round and the teeth more precisely shaped, Harley-Davidson purchased a new machine that shaved the gears to their final shape with greater precision, reducing runout and "high spots," which the company claimed reduced operating noise and made the engine's overall operation smoother.

Oiling System Updates

Another common source of oil leakage was the banjo-type oil fittings that secured the oil lines to the oil tank, especially the under-tank oil feed line fitting that was integral with the drain valve on the 1937 models. Continuing the theme of "cleaner" for 1938, Harley-Davidson moved the oil feed line fitting to the back of the oil tank's right side and changed the oil tank's oil-line fittings to better sealing compression-type fittings. This new tank is correct for 1938 and 1939 and is again painted black. Of course, the oil line fittings were also updated for the compression-type connections.

To improve breather action and help prevent clogging of the breather line in cold weather, the vent line from the oil tank to the crankcase was increased in size from 1/4 inch to 3/8 inch.

For 1938, the rear brake was again substantially modified. The backing plate was given a larger reinforcement plate, and the shoe pivot was replaced by a cup bearing that clamped both shoes together at the rear. The frame and forks were also made stouter for a better-handling machine. Note the rear stand. The old stand was half-round in section; the new stand was stamped with a channel down each leg and was lighter and cheaper to produce. *Copyright Harley-Davidson Michigan, Inc.*

The oil pump was updated for use with the diaphragm-type oil-pressure switch that was introduced with the new oil-pressure indicator light housed in the instrument cover (more on this later). The major modification to the pump was that the boss surrounding the sensing hole was lengthened to allow clearance for the switch. This style of oil pump was used only for 1938. The switch breaks the oil pressure indicator light circuit when the oil pressure reaches 3 psi, shutting off the indicator light. This switch threads into an adapter, which threads into the oil-pressure-sensing-hole boss on the oil pump. The switch is correct for 1938–1947, but this specific adapter was used on the OHV models for 1938 (but also on later side-valve models).

Stiffer Frame

The new, stronger frame that had been introduced in 1937 was a vast improvement over 1936's willowy frame, but the 1937 frame still exhibited signs of flexing when ridden at its limits or when lugging a sidecar. And its relatively lightweight rear frame tubes and open slot on the left axle clip's brake stay were also thought to contribute to the rear-brake chatter.

For 1938, Harley-Davidson fitted their Big Twins with a revised frame that was markedly stouter than its predecessors. The following reinforcements were made: The frame strut that triangulates the frame between the backbone tube and the lower part of the steering-head forging was made of larger diameter tubing (1 inch instead of 7/8 inch), the rear tubes that connect the axle clip forgings to the front portion of the frame were made of heavier-gauge steel (14-gauge instead of 16-gauge), the seat-post braces were made of heavier-gauge steel and were 1/2 inch wider, the transmission mounting bracket and rear support were made of heavier-gauge steel, and the brake stay on the left axle clip has a cap brazed on to close the end of the brake-stay slot.

The frame's steering head was also improved with the addition of a lower self-aligning head cone that has a convex base. Over the 1938 production run, the forging hallmarks on the left side of the steering head were phased out, and all subsequent Knucklehead steering heads lacked these marks.

The frame's toolbox strap was also revised for 1938 — not to make it stiffer, but to make it easier and cheaper to manufacture. On the previous frame, the mounting bolts for the

The big change for 1938 was the new valve enclosures. Unlike the old cup-style covers used in 1936 and 1937, the new covers enclosed the rocker arms as well as the valve springs. These covers kept out dirt and water and kept the oil in far better than the old covers had. For 1938, the upper and lower covers were fastened together by roundhead screws with threaded screw plates below, rather than the individual nuts shown here. Return lines from the new covers were made larger in diameter than those on the cup-type covers; the new lines seldom plugged up, so the air fitting on the front rocker housing was omitted on 1938 and later motors. The rocker-shaft mounts show the larger reinforcement rib (which was cast integrally with the cooling fin to its left) that was introduced in 1937. In late 1938, the rocker-shaft mounts were made even stronger. *Copyright Harley-Davidson Michigan, Inc.*

toolbox were each inserted through a hole in the toolbox strap and threaded into holes in the rectangular plates spot-welded to the wheel side of the strap. On the 1938 frame, the spot-welded plates were replaced by swaged-on threaded fittings. These fittings were used on all subsequent frames.

Sometime during 1938 production, the frame was improved yet again when a new left axle-clip forging was phased into production. The new forging no longer needed the brazed-on cap to close the end of the open slot for the brake stay because the slot's end was not left open on the new forging. Left-axle-clip forgings with closed brake-stay slots were used on all subsequent Knucklehead frames.

Brake Updates

While certain inadequacies of the early frames may have exacerbated the previously mentioned problem of rear-brake chatter and squeal, the real solution to these problems was in updates to the rear brake itself. the company actually began these changes in 1937, but the measures taken were only partly successful, so Harley-Davidson finally got serious about fixing the problem on their 1938 models.

First, the company followed up on its recommendation in the Shop Dopes by shortening the rear brake

linings, which reduced the tendency for the brakes to chatter and self-energize, and made the brake more powerful by allowing more of the lining's surface area to contact the drum. The updated linings were used on all 1938–1947 Knuckleheads. Then, Harley-Davidson added a larger anchor-tab reinforcement plate to the inside surface of the backing plate to reduce its tendency to flex under braking load. The new reinforcement plate wraps 2/3 of the way around the flat part of the backing plate and is secured with 14 rivets. This reinforced backing plate was also used from 1938 through the end of Knucklehead production in 1947.

Early in the 1938 production run, "interconnected" brake shoes were fitted to the rear brake. The shoes were interconnected by a new, two-piece cup bearing on the redesigned pivot stud. The pivot pads of the shoes were made wider to fit the new inner bearing and included a raised, semi-circular boss around the circumference of the pad, over which the cup-shaped outer bearing piece was fitted, securing the pivot end of the two shoes together. A cotter pin was then inserted through a hole in the stud, securing the top cup of the bearing to the stud. Because the new bearing connected the shoes together, the upper spring was omitted. With these final changes, the Knucklehead rear brake had reached its final form, far smoother and quieter than ever before.

The front brakes were also refined for 1938 to improve power and reduce squealing. "Softer" metal was used in the manufacture of the front drum, and the shoes were lined with "Rex-Hide" material. And maintenance was made easier through the addition of a grease fitting on the backing plate to lubricate the center bushing.

Revised Instrument Panel and Speedometer

Long before 1938, car and motorcycle manufacturers had begun to realize that by making their machines more sophisticated and easier to operate, they could make them appeal to a new group of buyers who were not necessarily interested in, or knowledgeable about, mechanics. These buyers were not interested in tinkering with their machine—they just wanted reliable transport. To these new customers, finicky features such as ammeters and adjustable oiling for the valve gear were unnecessary anachronisms that at best only confused them with more information than they knew what to do with—and at worst were like an open mine shaft that lay in wait to entrap them.

Anticipating the next stage of this trend, but years ahead of standard practice in the automotive industry, Harley-Davidson made an unpopular but wise move in 1938, when it abandoned the ammeter and mechanical oil-pressure indicator in favor of what are today called "idiot lights."

The ammeter was an elegant device that had been a popular feature because it provided useful information about the condition of the motorcycle's charging system. So why would Harley-Davidson risk alienating their customers by deleting it and the less-useful, but charming mechanical oil indicator?

The most important reason was probably cost—the two gauges were far more expensive to manufacture than were indicator lights—but the new system brought with it some very real benefits: reduced complexity and vulnerability of the oiling and electrical systems.

The mechanical oil-pressure indicator had required a steel oil line that connected to the oil pump and was routed along the frame to the gauge. This routing protected the line well, but the potential was there for vibration to cause the line to crack or to abrade through, or for the connections to leak, with potentially catastrophic results for the engine. The new oil-pressure indicator light used a sensor switch on the oil pump and a wire to the indicator light. When oil pressure drops below 3 psi, the switch closes the circuit, lighting the indicator lamp and illuminating the red lens that covers the opening on the right, where the mechanical indicator was formerly mounted.

Similarly, the entire current of the electrical system had to be routed through the ammeter for it to operate. Again, the added wiring was well protected, but Murphy's Law sometimes wins out even over slim odds. Instead of current, the new indicator light responds to the voltage difference between the battery and the new third terminal on the generator cutout relay. When battery voltage is higher than generator voltage, current flows through the lamp and illuminates the green lens in the opening formerly occupied by the ammeter. When generator voltage reaches battery voltage, the light goes out. According to an ad in the October 1937 issue of *The Motorcyclist*, "The [instrument-panel] lights are distinctly arresting, even in the daytime."

In addition to the new indicator lights, the 1938 instrument-panel cover was given two other noteworthy modifications: the tripmeter-reset hole was replaced by a slot and a 3/8-inch hole was added on the left side for a police speedometer hand lock.

The new tripmeter-reset slot is covered by a solid (for nontripmeter models) or cutout (for tripmeter models) metal cover that is attached by two screws. The hand-lock hole is sealed by a clip-on cover on civilian models. The wiring underneath the cover was revised for the new indicator lights, and the horn and light-switch wiring were rerouted between handlebar switches and the instrument panel to eliminate chafing. The instrument cover was painted black on motorcycles ordered with the standard option groups or was chrome-plated on motorcycles ordered with the Deluxe Solo Group or the Chrome Plate Special.

The standard speedometer on the Knucklehead for 1938 was equipped with a tripmeter (based on the fact that all models had to be ordered with one of the option groups and all the option groups for the Knucklehead included the trip odometer). This speedometer looks like the earlier speedometer, except that hashmarks were added for the 2-mile-per-hour intervals between the numerals, which are spaced at 10-mile-per-hour intervals between 10 and 120. These new hashmarks replaced the 5-mile-per-hour hashmarks formerly used. This new speedometer is correct for 1938–1940 61s.

Some 61s may have been fitted with nontripmeter speedometers. If they were, they were equipped with the old-style speedometer with 5-mile-per-hour hashmarks because the speedometer with 2-mile-per-hour hashmarks was made only with the tripmeter.

Transmission and Clutch

At the start of the 1938 model year, a number of small, largely invisible changes were made to the Knucklehead transmission and clutch. These included a new starter cover; a larger, stronger clutch release finger and revised finger stud with a longer bushing; a higher oil-level communicating hole between the starter cover and the gear case (to keep foreign particles from entering the gear case); reinforced mainshaft second gear ("fully 75 percent" stronger, according to an ad in the October 1937 issue of *The Motorcyclist*); wider lugs on second-gear shifter clutch; wider lugs and beveled engaging surfaces on the fourth-gear shifter clutch; and a third-gear engaging clutch with more clearance from the side of the lugs. Externally, a revised clutch operating lever and a revised clutch-pedal spring were also introduced. The release lever is like the previous lever, except that the left end has only one slot (instead of two),

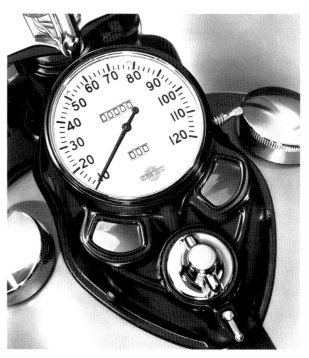

A revised speedometer and instrument-panel were introduced for 1938. The speedometer still had a 120-mile-per-hour face, but the hash marks were now at the intermediate 2-mile-per-hour intervals. The instrument panel shows the new "idiot" lights that replaced the ammeter and mechanical oil-pressure indicator in 1938. The left indicator (voltage) has a green lens, and the right indicator (oil-pressure) has a red lens. The skull-face panel with the colored lenses is correct for 1938 only. Standard instrument covers were painted black, but a chrome-plated cover was included in the Chrome Plate Special. *Copyright Harley-Davidson Michigan, Inc.*

A 1938 Knucklehead for the California Highway Patrol. Starting sometime during the middle of the model year, the Model 32E2R generator was introduced for radio-equipped police bikes. The 32E2R generator was a two-brush design that needed a separate voltage regulator, unlike earlier police generators, which were three-brush designs that did not need a separate regulator. The regulator is shown on this bike, just aft of the coil. California Highway Patrol bikes had the tool box on the left side to allow a rear-wheel siren on the right side. Note the arrowheads at the front of the pinstripes on the front fender. *Copyright Harley-Davidson Michigan, Inc.*

and the two pieces of the lever are welded together (rather than being brazed). This lever is Parkerized. The 1938 clutch-pedal springs are like the previous springs, except that they have only 19 coils (versus 22). These springs are painted black.

Most of the aforementioned changes were inconsequential in and of themselves, but they were necessary to implement a series of midyear changes that would constitute yet another attempt to fix two nagging problems with the Big Twin clutch: overheating and a weak throw-out bearing.

To make the clutch more resistant to overheating under police use, the clutch was given a new disc pack, an asbestos insulating gasket for the driving disc, a revised hub locknut, and new clutch springs. These parts were fitted to new machines after February 1, 1938, according to *Shop Dope No. 175*.

The new clutch-disc pack used two lined steel discs, two plain steel discs, one notched fiber disc, and one sprung disc.

The plain steel and notched fiber discs were the same type that had been used on previous clutches, but the lined discs and spring disc were new parts. Each lined disc consisted of a steel disc with notches around the outer circumference (to mate with the splines on the clutch drum) and fiber linings riveted onto each side of the disc. The new spring disc still has the L-slots on its outer circumference but lacks the spline notches on its inner circumference. This new disc pack was used through the 1940 model year, after which an all-new clutch made its debut.

Shorter, stiffer, and wound of thicker wire, the new clutch springs were protected from clutch heat by the new asbestos gasket, installed between the new clutch springs and the driving plate. Also added in this update were a longer clutch-hub locknut and a longer adjusting screw. All these parts were used through the 1940 model year.

The second big change was to introduce the second update to the throw-out bearing and a revised clutch pushrod for the new bearing. Curiously, the new pushrod was first fitted to new machines more than two weeks before the new bearing (after February 25, 1938, for the pushrod, and after March 8, 1938, for the bearing, according to *Shop Dope No. 174*). The 8-ball clutch throw-out bearing that had been used on Knuckleheads since late 1936 was replaced by a 10-ball throw-out bearing that was less prone to seizing. In the *Shop Dope*, dealers were instructed to retrofit any unsold machines with the new bearing and pushrod and to return for exchange any of these parts replaced under warranty.

This throw-out bearing was much larger and stouter than the previous bearing, but it still wasn't good enough and would be replaced the following year. Consequently, late in the 1938 production run, the starter cover was revised yet again, this time to include a reinforcing rib between the filler hole and the boss for the clutch-release-shaft opening—and for added clearance for the 25-ball clutch throw-out bearing that replaced the 10-ball throw-out bearing.

Finally, a new clutch pedal and bracket were introduced in midyear. The new clutch pedal is taller (5.75 inches versus 4.25 inches) but shorter in length (9 inches versus 9.125 inches) than the previous pedal. It, too, was only used for the latter part of 1938. The new clutch-pedal bracket is like the previous bracket, except that it is taller (9.75 inches versus 8 15/16 inches) and has four 0.75-inch holes in a square pattern on the bracket midsection instead of the former bracket's two holes. This bracket was used again for 1939.

J-Slot Air Cleaner

The optional air cleaner was revised for 1938 to make the cover easier to install or remove. It is no longer fastened to the backing plate by four screws—rather, four J-shaped slots in the new cover mate with four capped studs on the new backing plate to fasten the cover. This 6-inch-diameter air cleaner is correct for 1938–1940.

Forks and Handlebars

The 1938 forks were formed from stronger tubing to make them less prone to flexing. The fork was also fitted with wider front-fender mounting tabs, to make the tabs even more resistant to cracking from vibration. These forks, with the larger tubing and the old-style spring perches with the grease fittings on the front part of the spring perches (rather than on the sides), were used only in 1938.

Also for 1938, the bend on the handlebars was revised to allow more clearance for the rider's legs when the bars are turned. These bars are correct for 1938 to mid-1946. The individual bars are brazed to the cast center section on 1938 through mid-1945 Standard bars and on 1938–1942 Speedster bar. The bars are welded to the center section on late-1945 to mid-1946 Standard bars and 1943 to mid-1946 Speedster bars. Bars are painted black.

Redesigned Rear Stand

For 1938, a totally redesigned and lighter rear stand was introduced. Instead of being half-round, the legs on the new stand are stamped from sheet steel with rounded reinforcing channels. Although it was lighter, it was "amply strong for all requirements," according to the October 1937 issue of *The Enthusiast*. And the magazine continued, with a sentiment any rider could agree with. "Anyway, a motorcycle shouldn't be left on a stand—it was built to roam the highways and once you try one of these new '38 jobs you won't need a stand."

Other Small Changes

In addition to the more momentous changes already outlined, many other smaller changes were made, including the following: the Alemite grease fittings were replaced by Zerk-Alemite grease fittings; a third post was added to the generator cutout relay (correct for 1938–1947); the speedometer cable sheath was cadmium plated (rather than painted black); and the horn brackets and bolts were painted black (rather than being Parkerized).

Police-Bike Updates

Police bikes were given two major new convenience features for 1938. The first and most important was the magnetic speedometer hand stop available for mounting on the handlebar. With this new device, an officer could pace a car and press a button to freeze the speedometer needle at the pace speed. The second was a streamlined, polished-aluminum siren.

The steady increase in electric-powered police accessories, especially radios, was the impetus for the introduction of a new high-output police generator in mid-1938. The Model 32E2R had longer armatures and fields to produce more current than the standard Model 32E generator. The new generator was a 6-volt, two-brush generator that was used with a voltage regulator instead of with a cut-out relay.

Mature Design

After the hundreds of running changes implemented in 1936 and 1937, the design of the Knucklehead stabilized somewhat starting in 1938, as many of the modifications introduced that year fixed nagging problems well enough that they were not to be changed again during Knucklehead production. And for the first time the Knucklehead design lived up to its early promise. From 1938 on, the improved brakes, the use of indicator lights, and the finish on many of the parts remained unchanged, except on the rare wartime bikes, through the end of Knucklehead production in 1947.

1938 Production

After the 20 percent rise in sales that had so pleased Harley-Davidson in 1937, the 1938 sales were a big disappointment. Overall sales declined 30 percent—the result of flagging interest in the 45s, 74s, and 80s as the excitement initiated by their restyling in 1937 dissipated. The one ray of hope was that the 61 was even more popular, its sales rising more than 20 percent to 2,478. Of this total, 2,289 were ELs

and 189 were ESs. The 61s accounted for about 30 percent of overall Harley sales (up from 15 percent the year before), and this trend would continue in the following years.

Window to the World, 1939

For 1939, Europe was again the center of attention, and the march toward war continued. On March 14, Germany invaded Czechoslovakia. On April 7, Italy invaded Albania. Germany took the irrevocable final step on September 1, when it invaded Poland. On September 3, Britain and France declared war on Germany. That very day, the first American war casualties occurred when a German sub torpedoed and sunk the British passenger ship *Athenia*. Thirty Americans were killed. Even so, the United States declared neutrality two days later.

On September 17, Russia joined the fun and invaded Poland. The conquest complete, Germany and Russia partitioned Poland on September 28.

The big movie of the year was *Gone with the Wind*, starring Clarke Gable and Vivien Leigh. The movie was the longest and most expensive movie ever made and won 10 Academy Awards.

The starting gun sounded in the nuclear race when Enrico Fermi and John Dunning use a cyclotron to split uranium for the first time.

By the start of the 1939 production year, Harley-Davidson's bold new designs were really beginning to pay off. The September 1938 issue of *The Enthusiast* trumpeted the fact that, based on the 1937 registration lists, 67 percent of all motorcycles in the United States were Harley-Davidsons. And the new Harleys continued to make their mark on the tracks as well. A 1937 61 sidecar rig ridden by Robert Tinoco won the 24-hour Bol d'Or race in France on June 5, 1938. During the 24 hours, Tinoco horsed his sidecar rig around the 5-kilometer Montlhery over 400 times, logging 1,252.5 miles. This was the first time that the Bol d'Or was won by a sidecar rig. Knuckleheads also carried their riders to victory in the Southwestern TT Championship and several classes in the Jack Pine.

The 1939 Knucklehead

The OHV Big Twin model line for 1939 included only the high-compression 39EL Special Sport Solo and the medium-compression 39ES twin with sidecar gearing. In addition, a special police package was offered combining the medium-compression motor, the three-speed transmission, and medium gearing. All models were listed at a retail price of $435 (the same price as in 1937 and 1938) and had to be ordered with one of the option groups, at additional cost.

Two option groups for solos and one group for sidecar haulers were offered. The Standard Solo Group included

For 1939, Harley-Davidson introduced a new set of transmissions with a sliding-gear first (in three-speed and three-speed-with-reverse transmissions) or second (in four-speeds). This shifter gate for a three-speed-with-reverse transmission is on a 1939 EL owned and restored by Ron Lacey. On the four-speed gate, neutral was placed between second and third gear. The new transmissions were unpopular because the rider had to go through the nonsynchromesh second gear every time he shifted from neutral to first (on four-speeds), or through the nonsynchromesh first every time he shifted to reverse (three-speed-with-reverse).

the front safety guard, steering damper, stop light and switch, jiffy stand, trip odometer, front fender light and four-ply tires; the package listed for $15.50. The Deluxe Solo Group for 1939 was expanded, and included all the items in the standard group, plus ride control, colored shift knob, 6-inch round air cleaner, deluxe saddlebags, deluxe solo saddle, and Chrome Plate Special (which included chrome-plated handlebars, headlamp, instrument panel, taillight cover, relay cover, exhaust-pipe covers, and license-plate frame, fender strips, and stainless steel top fender strips). It listed for $47.00. The Standard Group for sidecar or commercial motorcycles listed for $14.00 and included a front safety guard, a steering damper, stop light and switch, trip odometer, fender light, and four-ply tires. It is interesting to note that the three-speed transmission with reverse gear was no longer included in the package.

Styling Changes

Changes for 1939 took Knucklehead styling to heights it had not reached since 1936, and would never reach again. Elements of the new style that made it so stunning included the new paint scheme, streamlined "cat's-eye" instrument panel, "boattail" taillight, and new stainless steel fender trim.

New Paint

With the possible exception of the 1936 scheme, the paint scheme introduced for 1939 is the most handsome scheme ever used on a Harley-Davidson Big Twin, in my opinion. Like

For 1939 another new instrument panel was introduced. The new panel was nicknamed the "cat's-eye" because of the almond-shaped windows for the generator and oil warning lights. Shadows highlight the V-shaped ridge that ends just aft of the restyled speedometer-light knob (which was also new for 1939). Although the cat's-eye cover was used through 1946, this V is only apparent on covers through model-year 1942. The disc-shaped light knob with the domed top was also used through 1942.

the 1936 scheme, the 1939 paint scheme was again two-tone, but this time the contrasting panels were on the sides of the gas tanks, rather than on the fenders. From a side view, the top edge of the panel continues the long diagonal line of the frame, from the steering head to the axle clips. From a front view, the top lines of the panels are seen to curve downward and toward the center of the bike in a V shape. A pinstripe accentuates the curved top line of the panel. The art deco tank transfer was used for the last time with the new tank panels.

Standard paint colors for 1939 were Airway Blue with white panels, black with ivory panels, and Teak Red with black panels. Police models were available in Police Silver with black stripes.

"Cat's-Eye" Instrument Cover

A restyled instrument cover added to the impact of the new tank panels. This new cover is longer and more streamlined than the previous cover and has a pronounced V-shaped ridge aft of the ignition-switch hole. The rectangular apertures for the warning lights were replaced by cat's-eye-shaped openings, giving rise to the nickname of this dash. Lenses over these openings were green and red.

Also restyled was the speedometer-light switch knob at the rear of the instrument panel. The 1937–1938 barbell-shaped knob was replaced by a disc-shaped knob, slightly rounded on top, with a knurled edge. It was cadmium plated. This instrument panel and speedo-light knob are correct for 1939–1942.

Rather than being painted black or chrome plated like previous covers had been, the 1939 cover was painted to match the color of the tank top and fenders, adding further to the distinctive new look. As the September 1938 issue of *The Enthusiast* bragged: "From front to rear there is a continuous flow of color!" Chrome-plated instrument panels were optional.

"Boattail" Taillight

For 1939, the small "beehive" taillight was replaced by a larger, more streamlined assembly. It was dubbed the "boattail" because its shape evoked the image of the sterns used on the streamlined muscleboats of the era. Standard taillight bodies were painted the color of the fenders, but chrome-plated bodies were available. This taillight is correct for 1939–1941 (in 1942 the taillight unit was only slightly revised).

The rear fender was revised for 1939 to omit the taillight shroud that had been necessary for the old-style taillight, and to add mounting holes for the new taillight and stainless steel trim pieces.

Fender Trim

Icing on the whole 1939 styling cake was the bright stainless steel strip along the top of each fender valance. These trim strips are correct for 1939–1942 and late 1946 through 1947.

The final styling change of note was a nod back to the 1936 Knuckle. In 1936, the patent decal was on the toolbox cover. In 1937 and 1938 two were fitted, one on each side of the oil tank. For 1939, the patent decal was once again on the toolbox—but for 1939 only. For 1940 and later it was fitted only to the left side of the oil tank.

Engine Updates

Several subtle changes were made to the exterior of the 1939 engine. Primer cups were no longer offered as an option, so the primer-cup bosses on the cylinder heads were not drilled and tapped for the cups. Parker-Kalon self-tapping screws and unthreaded lower screw plates were used to fasten the rocker covers' top caps. Neoprene-covered spark plug wires were introduced.

A plate with date markings was added just forward of the casting number on the left crankcase. Intake manifold and plumber-nut finish was changed to cadmium plate (instead of nickel plate). A drain screw was added to the carburetor's float bowl, and because this was the last year

A prototype of the 1939 Knucklehead. New features for 1939 that did not make it onto this prototype include the stainless steel fender side trim strips (note that they are painted in on this bike) and the 1937–1938 style of speedometer-light knob. The photo does show the 1939-only deluxe solo saddle and saddlebags. *Copyright Harley-Davidson Michigan, Inc.*

the Linkert M-5 was fitted to the Knucklehead, it is a one-year-only carburetor. And the adapter base for the oil-pressure switch was revised, which resulted in a reversion to the 1936–1938-style oil-pump body. Late in the production run, the rocker housing was revised to incorporate a casting date plate and to thicken the casting in the area around the intake pushrod hole.

Internally, a redesigned one-piece pinion shaft was fitted. The 1936–1938 pinion shaft was a two-piece shaft with the helically cut drive gear for the oil pump machined into the outer shaft stub and the pinion gear press-fit on the shaft. Over time, the joint between the two stub shafts would incrementally wear, allowing flex in the shaft, which resulted in slight misalignment of the gears.

For 1939, the new shaft was machined from a solid bar with six splines running along the axis of the shaft, and the oil-pump gear was a separate piece. The pinion shaft assembly consisted of a one-piece pinion shaft, an oil-pump gear spacer, an oil-pump drive gear, a spring, and a pinion gear. The new pinion gear for the oil pump is larger in diameter (1 3/16 inches versus 1 inch) and is splined, but still has five teeth. This one-piece shaft kept the gears in almost perfect alignment. It was used through 1953. The pinion gear was used through 1950.

Mating with the pinion shaft's new, larger-diameter drive gear for the oil pump is a new, smaller-diameter gear (1 3/8 inches versus 1 9/16 inches) on the oil pump's driveshaft. The result is that the oil pump spins much faster, bringing the system up to operating pressure at lower rpm and generating higher overall oil pressure and flow. Unfortunately, this was a mixed blessing. A quicker rise to operating pressure was certainly advantageous, but the increased flow that came with it resulted in oil-fouled spark plugs and increased oil consumption at low rpm.

To solve the problem, a new, relief-valve spring was introduced early in the production run that allows the relief valve to open at 4–6 psi, venting the excess oil into the gear case, from which it is returned to the oil tank by the scavenge pump. This went a long way toward reducing the severity of the over-oiling problem at low rpm, but it was really just a band-aid fix that brought its own penalty—it also limited the oil pressure available at high rpm and wasted much of the output of the pump. Harley's engineers must have been satisfied with it, though, because the next attempt to fix the problem would not occur until the 1941 model year.

The old-style straight crankcase breather pipe that had been used since 1936 was replaced by a new pipe with a double elbow that bends forward and then to the left, through a hole in a revised inner primary cover. Inside the primary enclosure, a separate oil deflector attached to the end of the breather tube deflects the oil onto the primary chain. The new inner primary cover is like the previous cover, except that a new hole for the revised crankcase breather pipe was added to the bulge at the rear of the front reinforcing rib, a dimple appeared at the location of the former crankcase breather-pipe hole, and the stamped-in boss around the transmission mainshaft hole was made larger.

Standard Knuckleheads for 1939 were dressy machines, but Eldon Brown's machine is dressed up even more, with the disc wheels, white-wall tires (which were not offered on new machines that year), spotlamps, stainless steel trim strips for the top of the fenders (included in the Chrome Plate Special), and an accessory rear safety guard. This is a beautiful restoration, but a few parts were incorrectly cadmium plated when they should have been Parkerized, including the front brake cam lever and brake-mounting hardware, the rear brake rod, the stand hardware, and rear axle and nut.

Rounding out the motor changes for the start of 1939 were pistons that were reinforced with thicker metal behind the third ring grooves, and a revised screen on the breather valve. Improved valve springs were also introduced.

Nonadjustable Rocker-Arm Oiling

But another major change to the engine was made during the production year. Continuing the trend toward simplification and making their machines "idiot-proof," Harley-Davidson finally got rid of adjustable rocker oiling in 1939. With the advent of the fully enclosed rocker covers in 1938, the consequences of over-adjustment were no longer as critical because the oil remained inside the covers rather than spraying out to coat bike and rider—yet the risk of squeaking valves and accelerated valve-gear wear from under-adjustment remained.

The solution was to fit all new machines after 39EL1902 with new rocker arms and rocker shafts, with fac-

tory-set oiling. The new rocker shafts lack the previous shaft's oil grooves, and the central oil passage ends at two oil holes on the bearing surface, near the right end. The new rocker arms are like the previous arms, except that the oil passage to the valve-pad stem ends at a hole on the side of the stem, rather than under the stem. With these new parts, top-end oiling problems were cured at last.

Frame and Forks

The 1939 61 OHV frame was the same as the previous frame, except that the steering head was fitted with a self-aligning upper cone to match the self-aligning lower cone that had been introduced in 1938.

The 1939 fork was made easier to service by moving the grease fittings on the spring perch from in between the headlight bosses to the sides of the perch, where they are easily accessible. (The original grease-fitting bosses between the headlight bosses remain, but they are not drilled for the fittings.) To improve the ride, lighter cushion springs were fitted on forks for solo machines. Forks for sidecar machines were fitted with the same cushion spring, but an additional cushion spring was fitted in place of the buffer spring. This fork is correct for 1939 through early 1942.

Sliding-Gear Transmission

Even though the sliding-clutch four-speed, three-speed, and three-speed-with-reverse transmissions introduced on the 1936 Knucklehead had proved to be just about the only major system that was trouble-free, Harley-Davidson introduced a whole new set of Big Twin transmissions for 1939 that incorporated old-style sliding gears for second gear on the four-speed and for first gear on the three-speeds—a seemingly retrograde step. The September 1938 issue of *The Enthusiast* claimed that the change "will make for easier, smoother shifting." In fact, the opposite was true.

So what was the real reason for the change? Second gear in the four-speed and first gear in the three-speeds was the gear used most by police and commercial users, and the gears didn't stand up to such constant use as well as they should have. These users were in the minority, however, and the more sport-minded riders who were in the majority didn't care for the delay in shifting caused by the sliding gear. In a compromise Harley-Davidson hoped would satisfy both groups, the sliding-gear second was used only for 1939, while the pair of three-speeds kept the sliding-gear first through the end of Knucklehead production in 1947.

The new transmissions had a revised shift pattern, so the shift gates were revised. On the sliding-gear four-speed, the neutral position was between second and third (rather than between first and second), so the markings on its shift gate were changed accordingly. Depth of the gate's high-gear notch (fourth on four-speeds; third on three-speeds) was reduced by half to ease shifting out of high. This four-speed transmission gate was a 1939-only part. The gate for the three-speeds was used through 1946.

The final changes to the 1939 transmissions were a new starter clutch designed to work with the new 25-ball throw-out bearing (discussed in the next section), shifter fingers revised to include rollers, and a midyear shifter-cover revision to include a cast-in date mark on the inside. These changes were carried forward to the next year's transmissions.

25-Ball Throw-Out Bearing

After numerous updates that ultimately proved unsatisfactory (most recently in mid-1938), the throw-out bearing was finally fixed for real in 1939. The all-new throw-out bearing is much larger than the old bearing and has 25 ball bearings instead of the former bearing's 10. The bearing is cone-shaped, tapering toward the redesigned clutch release fingers, and its retainer has four scooper cups to supply lubricant. A new starter clutch was also fitted. The designs of the bearing and release fingers were so sound that they were used on Harley-Davidson Big Twin transmissions into the 1970s.

The 25-ball throw-out bearing may be fitted to some earlier machines because a kit was released in the spring of 1939

The new "boat-tail" taillight for 1939 did not use the metal shroud that had been used on the 1936–1938 "beehive" taillight. The new taillight had a red lens at the rear and a frosted lens on top to illuminate the license plate, which mounts to a separate bracket. Standard taillight covers were painted the color of the fender, but a chrome-plated cover was included as part of the Chrome Plate Special.

to allow use of the bearing on earlier machines. As described in *Shop Dope No. 191*, the kit included a new starter cover, release finger, release-finger shaft, thrust bearing, starter clutch, and oil deflector, and retailed for $7.50.

Clutch Pedal and Springs

The clutch footpedal was revised in 1939 by moving the stud for the clutch rod one inch upward on the side of the pedal's vertical center section. The hole in the pedal for the lower stud position remained on the new pedal. This pedal was Parkerized and is correct for 1939 and 1940.

Clutch-pedal balancing springs were also revised. The springs are like the previous springs, except that one end is no longer bent into a hook. Instead, it tapers and connects to a separate wire loop. These springs were painted black and are correct for 1939–1942.

Another California Highway Patrol bike, this one a 1939 model. Note that the toolbox is now mounted sideways, below the radio, but that the special strap for mounting the toolbox on the left side of the frame remains. *Copyright Harley-Davidson Michigan, Inc.*

Brakes

The 61's front brake received several improvements for 1939. The front linings were shortened to reduce chatter and the tendency to self-energize, as the rear shoes had been in 1938. To accommodate the new linings, the shoes were drilled in different places. These new linings were used through the end of the Knucklehead line in 1947.

To make the task of lubing the front brake shackle easier, the grease fitting on the fork end was relocated so that it points rearward when the shackle is installed. On the shackle stud, the screw-slot head was replaced by a hex head. Both shackle and stud were one-year-only parts.

The final change to the front brakes was the addition of a larger cable oiler on the cable's coil. The oiler has a Parkerized body and a spring-loaded plunger. The new oiler was fitted through 1947 production.

Foot controls for the rear brake were also revised. The brake pedal is about 1/4-inch shorter than the previous pedal and is slightly reshaped. This pedal body remained in production through 1947. The pedal was Parkerized. To simplify assembly, the pedal support was revised with a peened-on pivot stud (rather than bolted-on).

New Fuel Filter

Though the old-style fuel filter, with its side connection for the fuel line, had worked fine, Harley-Davidson replaced it for 1939 with an all-new filter that had the gas line connection at the bottom. To clean the strainer, the fuel line must be disconnected, allowing the gasoline to drain out over the cleaner's hands and onto the engine case and exhaust pipes. It should be obvious why the design was disliked. Even so, it remained in production through 1941. A tapered-flare-nut fitting connected the gas line to the filter.

An unrestored 1939 sidecar rig owned by Dave DeMartini, proprietor of Northwest Custom Cycle, in Snoqualmie, Washington. DeMartini has owned this bike since 1972. After he and his wife, Joanne, were married in 1976, they drove away from the church on this machine.

Eldon Brown's 1939 Knuckle shines from any angle. The wheels were made by welding the discs and rim onto a rider's H-D hubs sent in at the time of order. Wheels with 5.50 x 16 General Dual-10 tires, tubes, and flaps sold for $59. Shipping weight was listed as 94 pounds.

The 1939 transmissions came with numerous internal changes, some of which were improvements and some of which were definitely retrograde. Among the improvements was yet another (the fourth in four years) throw-out bearing, shown in this photo as the truncated-cone-shaped part inside the kickstarter cover. The new bearing for 1939 was much larger and had 25 ball bearings instead of 10. This new bearing was finally strong enough; it would be used on H-D Big Twins for more than 35 years. *Copyright Harley-Davidson Michigan, Inc.*

A 1939 EL owned and restored by Ron Lacey of British Columbia. In addition to the black-with-ivory-panels scheme shown on this bike, standard colors included Airway Blue with white panels, Teak Red with black panels, and police silver with black striping.

Brown Saddles

The 1939 standard solo saddle was like the previous saddle, except that the leather was rhino-russet-grain horsehide instead of black cowhide. This seat is correct for 1939 only.

The 1939 deluxe solo seat was also covered in brown horsehide, but it featured a three-piece leather skirt. The rear part of the skirt is shorter than the longer side-skirt lobes for clearance between the skirt and the fender. The two side skirts are sewn to the center skirts. At the center of the rear skirt is a trim piece that has a floral design under a clear piece of convex glass. Near the lobed tip of each side skirt is a leather, two-layer rosette with a short leather tassel, matching those on the optional saddlebags. This seat is also correct for 1939 only.

Sportier Front Safety Guard

As befits its name, the front safety guard was meant to prevent damage to bike and rider in the event of a crash. But the early safety guard was a safety hazard to the really brave riders of the day who tried to test the limits of the bike's cornering clearance. When it touched down, the stout tubing of the safety guard gave a sideways jolt to the bike that was not at all unlike that given when a forgotten sidestand touches down.

For 1939, Harley-Davidson revised the bend on the guard to address the problem. The new guard was almost identical to the old, except that it is bent so that it loops a bit farther forward (instead of more nearly straight out to the sides), which reduces the effective width of the crashbar, resulting in slightly more cornering clearance. The September 1938 issue of *The Enthusiast*

Obviously, the springs should not be chromed, but this photo does show two subtle new features of the 1939 and later machines: the grease fitting sticking out of each side of the rigid leg's spring perch and the larger oiler on the front brake coil (shown just above the top nut of the forks).

LEFT: Eldon Brown restores his machines with great care and rides them little so they stay pristine.

reassured riders that "you can sure lay the Big Twins over on the curves now." This new safety guard was fitted for 1939 and 1940.

1939 Production

Overall sales of Harley-Davidson motorcycles made a slight gain in 1939 of 1.6 percent—nothing to rejoice over, but far more satisfactory than the 30 percent decline in sales in 1938. Once again, the 61 was the star of the line-up, and it was also the only bulwark preventing another sales catastrophe. Sales of the Knucklehead increased by almost 20 percent to 2,909. Of this total, 2,695 were ELs and 214 were ESs.

Since its shaky debut, the 61 OHV had been refined to become the great American motorcycle of its era. Among American production motorcycles, it offered unmatched speed, sophistication, and power, and it even stood up well against limited-production specialty machines such as the Broughs, Vincent-HRDs, and Crockers. No longer was the Knucklehead more delicate, leaky, or trouble-prone than its peers—even those with the much simpler and less powerful flathead motor. As a result, its sales grew steadily between 1936 and 1939, while sales of its less sophisticated—read, flathead—stablemates and competitors were stagnant. By the end of the 1939 model year, the sexy 61 had clearly proved the Harleys and the Davidsons right in their belief that OHVs were the future. And a bright future it would be!

CHAPTER THREE

1940-1946

The Big Port Engine

Nothing jump-starts an economy like a good war or preparations for one. And the United States had been gearing up for several years. On September 1, 1939, as Harley-Davidson began assembling its 1940 models, Hitler took the final, irrevocable step toward world war when his troops invaded Poland.

The U.S. economy really came alive in the fall of 1939, as defense spending rose and factories struggled to meet the demand for war materiel for the United States and Allied forces. Ever eager to do its part, Harley-Davidson was already hard at work designing the WLA and other military motorcycles that kept it busy during the war years.

The United States was not yet in the war, however, so H-D did not neglect its civilian line-up. For 1940, the company introduced the first extensive revamp of its crown jewel, the 61 OHV, since the design had stabilized for model year 1937.

Window to the World, 1940

Not relishing the job but realizing that the coming conflict would require a steady, experienced hand at the helm, FDR ran for an unprecedented third term as president. In November, he won in an electoral landslide.

After the war ended, civilian production gradually resumed. The first bikes built were like the few built during the war—very plain, with almost no chrome- or cad-plated parts and limited paint selections. Like almost all wartime-through-1946 bikes, this one was updated with many of the normally plated parts when it was restored, rather than with all the Parkerized parts. It was also given a nonstandard two-tone paint scheme using the two regularly offered colors available early that year: red and gray. On February 5, 1946, the gray color was replaced by Skyway Blue. It is owned by Larry Engesether of Wisconsin.

In Britain, Winston Churchill replaced Neville Chamberlain as prime minister and became the symbol of British resolve to fight and win.

On the continent, the Nazi blitzkrieg rolled on, overrunning Denmark, Norway, Holland, Belgium, Luxembourg, and France. Soon after, the Battle of Britain began as German planes daily attacked London.

Relations between the United States and Japan continued to deteriorate as the year went on, and accelerated in July when FDR banned export to Japan of scrap metal and oil.

FDR vowed to turn America into the "Arsenal of Democracy." Early in the year he asked for and got the funds to build 50,000 warplanes. In July, he asked for and got $4 billion for new Navy ships. In November, he convinced Congress to agree to allocate half the military production to England.

Realizing late in the year that it takes soldiers—not just planes, tanks, and ships—to win a war, Congress passed the Selective Service Act, instituting the first peacetime draft for the United States.

Fred Ham, the California bike cop who set the 24-hour record in 1937 on a Knucklehead, was killed on December 9 when a car crossed in front of his bike during a high-speed chase.

The 1940 Knucklehead

The OHV Big Twin model line for 1940 included only the high-compression 40EL Special Sport Solo and the medium-compression 40ES twin with sidecar gearing. For the second year, a special police package was offered, but for 1940 it included only the three-speed transmission and medium gearing, not the medium-compression motor. All models were

LEFT: For 1940 the Knucklehead was restyled and given updated cylinder heads. This unrestored machine is owned by Wayne Pierce, Sr. and Wayne "Whiz" Pierce, Jr. of Pierce Harley-Davidson in DeKalb, Illinois.

A major part of the restyle was the switch to metal tank badges, replacing the art deco transfers that had been used since 1936. For 1940, the two tanks were interconnected by a balance tube from the right tank to the left. Individual petcocks for each tank were replaced by a single "instant-on" fuel valve that gave the rider quick access to the main and reserve fuel supplies by turning a knob on the top of the left tank, just to the left of the speedometer.

listed at a retail price of $430 ($5 less than in 1939) and had to be ordered with one of the option groups, at additional cost.

For 1940, the option groups were reshuffled and a new one was added. The Standard Solo Group was no longer offered, its place as the most basic trim package taken by the new Utility Solo Group. Included in this package were only the most rudimentary "options," such as front safety guard, steering damper, jiffy stand, and four-ply tires, which should have been included in the base price, but were $11 extra. The basic package for sidecar and package-truck machines was renamed the Utility Group, and it included the front safety guard, steering damper, and four-ply tires for $8.50.

The mid-level option package, also new, was the Sport Solo Group, which included a front safety guard, steering damper, jiffy stand, air cleaner, trip odometer, fender light, chrome rims, chrome exhaust-pipe covers, colored shift ball, and four-ply tires, all for $22.50.

For a really "doggy" machine, the Deluxe Solo Group was offered. This group ($46.00) included a front safety guard, steering damper, jiffy stand, air cleaner, ride control, trip odometer, fender light, deluxe saddlebags, deluxe solo saddle, colored shift ball, four-ply tires, and Chrome Group (chrome-plated rims, handlebars, headlight, instrument panel, relay cover, exhaust-pipe covers, license frame, and top fender strips).

Styling Changes

With model year 1940 came the first major restyle of the Knucklehead. Unlike earlier restyles, this one was more than paint deep. The machine's look was modernized through use of revised gas tanks, new tank emblems, all-new footboards, and a reshaped toolbox. Overall, the restyle could be called "speed-lined and streamlined." Like the styling cues set on the first series of Knuckleheads, those set in 1940 would be resurrected by the company in later years, most recently and conspicuously on the 1997 Springer Heritage Softtail.

Tanks and Fenders

The most obvious styling changes were the new paint scheme and tank emblems. Gone with the 1930s were the art deco tank transfers that had fit the mood of the prior decade so well, replaced by teardrop-shaped emblems in chrome-plated stamped brass. The company name is debossed down the centerline of the emblems, and the name is framed above and below by a pair of tapered "speed-lines." Speed-lines are painted black, and letters are painted red. This emblem is correct for 1940 to 1946. Each gas tank was fitted with a single, horizontal mount for the tank emblem.

Also gone were the tank panels that had made the 1939 61 so distinctive. Instead, tanks were painted one solid color, except for a pinstripe that starts just forward of the tank badge and sweeps up and back toward the aft end of the tank before jogging forward horizontally, ending several inches aft of the tank emblem. Overall, the pinstripe suggests a projected shadow that frames the emblem perfectly.

Standard colors were black with Flight Red stripe, Clipper Blue with white stripe, Squadron Gray with Bittersweet stripe, Flight Red with Black stripe, and Police Silver with black stripe (police only). Fenders were painted the same color as the tanks, and were fitted with the same classy stainless steel trim stripes as in 1939.

In addition to the tank emblem, the left tank features the "instant-reserve" fuel valve, an innovative feature that controls the flow of fuel from both tanks through one valve, replacing the separate petcocks that had been standard since 1936. This new valve makes it much easier for the rider to turn the fuel on and off—and especially to access the reserve fuel supply without burning his or her hands on the cylinder head. The valve mechanism is fully enclosed within the tank, with only the knob visible on the top of the tank, just to the left of the speedometer. Unscrew the knob to the top of the threads to access the main gas supply. Lift the knob up and away from the tank to access the reserve. A spring-loaded neoprene backing holds it in the reserve position. Reserve capacity is 3/4 gallon.

Left and right fuel tanks are interconnected by a coiled balance line that attaches to a nipple fitting on the front underside of the right tank and the fuel valve on the left tank. They act as one tank when the bike is upright and draining. Unfortunately, they still act as one when the bike is on its side-stand and is being filled. If the right tank is filled first, the gas will flow through the balance tube and fill the left tank, too—and this tendency sometimes results in a bit of Harley hilarity. At their first fill, neophyte Knucklehead riders often get a lesson they'll never forget when, after completely filling the right tank, they then pull off the left tank's gas cap. Their eyes bug out as fuel unexpectedly gushes out and over the hot

A late-1940 police Knucklehead. Two different gear case covers were fitted to 1940 Knuckleheads, and both have eight 1/4-inch-wide cooling fins. Early- and mid-1940 Knuckleheads came with a thick, sand-cast cover with a somewhat rough surface texture and a flat surface behind the cooling fins. The late-1940 style is shown on this machine. It is die cast, giving it a much smoother texture, and it is thinner than the earlier gear cover. Because it is thinner, the surface behind the cooling fins shows the diagonal boss for the breather-tube passage and the circular boss for the pinion bushing. *Copyright Harley-Davidson Michigan, Inc.*

engine of their new mount. It's pretty comical watching them trying to decide whether to run for their lives from what they imagine will be an imminent explosion, or run for the nearest paper towel to wipe the gas off the bike's paint.

Like the balance line, the fuel line is an all-new part. It runs unbranched from a tapered-flare-nut fitting at the tank's fuel valve to a tapered-flare-nut fitting at the bottom of the fuel filter. This gas line was used only for 1940 and 1941; in 1942, a revised line was fitted for a side-feed gas filter.

Ribbed Gear Cover

After four years of plain, flat, featureless gear-case covers, the gear-case cover was revised for 1940 to harmonize with the flowing lines of the rest of the motorcycle. The new, sand-cast gear cover is internally the same as the

previous cover (with cast-in baffle plate and breather tunnel), but the outside of the casting was given eight 1/4-inch-wide horizontal "cooling" fins. "Strength is added and heat is dissipated," according to the September 1939 issue of *The Enthusiast*.

Most 1940 machines were fitted with these sand-cast covers, but the cover was revised again very late in the production season, and the very last 1940 machines were fitted with a completely redesigned cover. This cover is die-cast, resulting in a smoother appearance. Externally, bulges for the breather-tube passage and pinion-bushing boss project beyond the base surface of the cover, but not beyond the level of the ribs. Internally, a riveted-on baffle plate replaces the cast-in baffle plate used on the previous cover, and the word "ALCO" and the number "97-403" are cast in relief. This cover is correct through 1947.

This bike is reported to be an original-paint machine, which means it must have been special ordered in this color. Standard colors for 1940 were Clipper Blue with white stripe, Flight Red with black stripe, Squadron Grey with Bittersweet stripe, Black with Flight Red stripe, and Police Silver with black stripe. This bike has most of the features of the Chrome Group for 1940, which was part of the Deluxe Solo Group and included chrome-plated rims, handlebar, headlamp, instrument panel, relay cover, exhaust-pipe covers, license frame, and top fender decoration. This machine also carries the "airplane-style" speedometer that is correct for 1941–1946 Knuckleheads. The correct tripmeter-equipped speedometer for 1940 is the "white-face" 120-mile-per-hour speedometer with 2-mile-per-hour hash marks that was introduced in 1938.

Teardrop Toolbox

Continuing the trend toward a more streamlined look for the new decade, the 1940 models were given a racy new tool box to replace the boxy, rectangular toolbox used on the 1936–1939 61. The new toolbox is a stream-lined teardrop with five ribs embossed on the cover. "The ribbing on the toolbox harmonizes with the new lines on the crankcase and adds plenty of sweep and dash to the entire motorcycle," gushed the September 1939 issue of *The Enthusiast.*

Unlike the previous tool box, this one mounts horizontally, wide end forward, the taper of the box's top line gracefully following the line of the top right rear frame tube. The cover is secured by a lock, and the toolboxes is painted black. This style of toolbox is correct for 1940 1947 Knuckles and on the Panheads through 1957.

For 1940 only, the toolbox bracket is riveted to the frame's tool-box strap. On 1941 and later machines, the bracket is a separate piece.

Half-Moon Footboards

After the toolbox, the last real square corners to be rounded were the footboards, which also were redesigned for a more streamlined effect. The new footboards are D-shaped and have redesigned rubber floorboard mats riveted on. With only minor changes over the years, these footboards were standard on all Harley-Davidson Big Twins through 1965. Footboards are Parkerized for 1940–1942 and have rubber mats.

At the same time Harley-Davidson updated the footboards, they cured a nagging problem in the clutch-pedal mechanism. On pre-1940 clutch-pedal assemblies, the pivot-bearing cover rattled almost constantly because it was only loosely held in

For 1940, "half-moon" footboards replaced the rectangular footboards that had been used on Harley-Davidsons since 1914. The half-moon footboards soldiered on almost as long as the rectangular boards had, until they were replaced on the 1966 Shovelhead Electra Glide with a new, semirectangular design.

place by the pedal bracket's spring stud and spring. For 1940, a revised clutch-pedal bracket was fitted. Its spring stud was threaded for a new nut to firmly fasten the cover in place. The bearing cover was revised to omit the "step" that had been embossed around the spring-stud hole, and the hole was increased to 27/64 inch in diameter (rather than 5/16 inch). The cover was painted black, and the bracket was Parkerized.

Fat Tires

It doesn't matter whether they're on a Deuce Coupe hotrod, a lifted four-by-four truck, or a 1940 Harley—fat tires can give the meekest machine the aura of performance. Usually, the aura is all you really get, but the millions of "sticker-package" performance cars sold during the 1970s proved convincingly that the look is all most people really wanted anyway. The bike we're talking about here, the 1940 Knucklehead, was one of the early pioneers of this trend, but it was an accidental trend-setter. And actually, H-D was following the lead of aftermarket companies such as Wolfe and Goulding. G. R. Wolfe was first, designing a special disc wheel and talking General into building a special 5.50x16-inch tire

called the Dual 10, with "squeegee action" tread, and offering them for sale in the April 1938 issue of *The Motorcyclist*. The Wolfe Safety Wheels were custom-built on the customer's hubs and a set of wheels, tires, tubes, and flaps sold for $59. They were heavy, though; shipping weight was listed as 94 pounds! These wheels are shown on Eldon Brown's 1939 61 in this chapter.

For 1940, fat 16-inch tires were made optional on all Harley-Davidson models. While style was almost certainly considered, the fatter tires were fitted for a more functional reason: the fatter tires could be run at lower pressure so that the sidewalls could flex more than those on the 18-inch tires, absorbing the effects of small road bumps and compensating somewhat for the lack of damping on the front fork and for the complete lack of suspension in the rear.

Problem was, the frame's 28-degree steering, head angle had been set up for the standard 18-inch tires, so machines fitted with the 16-inch tires didn't handle properly. At low speeds, the steering was heavy. And at high speed the front end gave poor feel and could easily go into a scary wobble on bumpy roads. Savvy riders cured the problem by having their frame "bumped"—bent using a frame jig and press, or by simply hitting the frame's backbone just behind the steering head with a heavy mallet—to increase the steering-head angle slightly. Harley-Davidson even recommended that its dealers resort to such measures to fix bikes with chronic handling problems, but I doubt the dealers really told their customers the disturbing details of the fix.

Despite the handling problems, most riders opted for the bigger tires, probably because they liked the look. But opinion was mixed on the looks at the time, and still is today. More traditional riders felt that the fat tires disrupted the OHV's sleek lines and were the ruin of a fine-handling machine. The factory liked what their customers liked, so fashion won out, and the 16-inch tires became standard the following year.

As alluded to earlier, the fat tires started a trend, and that trend came to be the great equalizer among American motorcycles, for Indian began fitting its machines with the fat tires in 1941, transforming their looks and ruining their handling forever, too.

A Few More Horses

Styling, schmyling, I say. The real changes for 1940 were all inside the motor. This was a bike for the new decade, after all, and Harley-Davidson intended to start the new era right. "Harley-Davidson engineers corralled a few more horses and packed them into the new 61 OHV motor," bragged the September 1939 issue of *The Enthusiast*. And all they had to

RIGHT: In addition to all the correct chrome bits included in the Chrome Group, this bike has many extra chrome-plated parts, including the primary cover and the rear chain guard. Like most 1940 Knuckleheads, this one was fitted with 5.00x16-inch tires, which first became optional for 1940. Fatter tires changed the look of the motorcycle substantially.

Like the footboards, the toolbox was restyled for 1940 from its old rectangular form to a more rounded, streamlined shape. The black air-cleaner cover shown is a war-time part; the optional air cleaner for 1940 was chrome plated.

do to get those extra horses was to open the gate a bit wider by enlarging the intake ports, intake manifold, and carburetor.

Large-Port Cylinders Heads

New head castings were introduced for 1940 with larger intake ports and a larger diameter threaded hole for the new, larger intake nipple for the new, larger manifold. Missing from the new casting was the boss for the primer cups, since the cups were no longer offered. Except for these changes, the head castings were like the 1939 castings. These head castings are correct for 1940 through 1947 civilian Knuckleheads (the few military OHVs built had a unique set of head castings with small ports on large-port castings).

Carburetor and Intake Manifold

The real key to opening the corral gate was the Linkert M-25 carburetor fitted to the 1940 Knucklehead. The M-25 is a 1-1/2-inch carburetor with a 1-5/16-inch venturi, replacing the venerable Linkert M-5 1-1/4-inch carb with a 1-1/16-inch venturi. Four bolts (instead of three) mount the new carburetor to a flange on the manifold. With its 1/4-inch-larger venturi, the M-25 added noticeably to the Knucklehead's top end, but at a cost in low-end power and throttle response, so it was used on the 61 only for 1940 (but it was also used on the early-1941 74-ci OHVs). In a cost-cutting move, the new carburetor was painted silver instead of being nickel plated.

Better performance was the goal, so the intake manifold was completely redesigned to carry the increased flow from the larger carburetor. Previous manifolds had been Y-shaped, but the 1940 manifold was reshaped to a T section, with 1 9/16-inch-diameter brass tubes (rather than 1-3/8-inch cast iron) in each section. The manifold's carburetor flange is drilled for four mounting bolts, and the cylinder-head ends have a smooth bushing surface. New, larger-diameter plumber nuts and brass bushings slide onto the bushing surfaces to fasten the manifold to the new, larger-diameter intake nipples. Manifold and plumber nuts were cadmium plated.

While the new, larger intake provided the gateway for more fuel-air mixture to flow from the carburetor to the intake ports, a flaw in its design also allowed air to leak in, resulting in backfires, misses, and poor performance. The problem was that the bushings and manifold were both made of brass. Time and vibration would make the bushing gall and seize on the manifold, ruining the seal. Because of this problem, the brass manifold was used for 1940 only; it would be cast iron starting in 1941.

Other Top-End Changes

To handle the increased horsepower produced by the new carburetor and intake tract, the cylinder castings were revised so that the tunnels for the head bolts extended

This air-brushed photo from the Harley-Davidson archives shows how the company would often have an older photo retouched to show new features, in this case the revised valve cover screws added in 1939 and the large-port heads introduced in 1940. This is essentially the same photo as the one printed in chapter 2, except that hex-head screws (Parker-Kalon self-tapping, introduced in 1939) were airbrushed over the round-head screws, the individual nuts for each screw were airbrushed out (screw plates were used), the rounded boss over the intake tract was airbrushed larger to show its size on the large-port heads, and the primer-cup boss was airbrushed out (it was deleted from the casting starting in 1940). The airbrush artist neglected to change one prominent feature, however. The rocker-shaft brackets shown were used only through about midyear 1938. The large-port heads were fed by a larger carburetor and intake manifold. *Copyright Harley-Davidson Michigan, Inc.*

through five cylinder fins, rather than through four. Except for this one change, the cylinders are unaltered. New head bolts, 5/16 inch longer than the superseded bolts, pass through the tunnels to fasten the heads to the cylinders. These cylinders and bolts were fitted for 1940–1947.

With the advent of fully enclosed rocker covers in 1938, problems of oil leaking out had been solved. But there was still the matter of over- or under-oiling of the intake valves. Too much, and the bike would suck oil in past the intake valve stem to smoke and foul the spark plugs. Too little, and the valves would squeak and wear.

The underoiling problem was solved when fixed oiling for the valve gear was introduced in mid-1939, but some individual engines were still prone to sucking in oil when used hard. This problem was finally solved on the 1940 engine by the use of revised guides for the intake valves. The new guides have a taper at the top that deflects oil spray away from the valve stem and also causes accumulated oil to flow away from the stem. The new guide was used only in the intake position and for 1940–1947.

To seal another source of oil seepage, the lower pushrod covers were redesigned for 1940 to have a flange at the bottom to rest on top of the lower cork seal (previous covers lacked the flange

and were pushed down inside the cork seal). To make removing the pushrod-cover retainer easier, the retainer was revised to have a small "handle," through which a small screwdriver blade could be inserted to pry out the retainer. The new lower cover and retainer were chrome plated. These parts are correct for 1940–1947 (except that they were Parkerized for 1943–1946).

Bottom-End Updates

The 61's bottom end was extensively revised for 1940 to strengthen it and to equalize the amount of oil reaching the two cylinder walls. The strength was provided by a beefier crankpin and bearing, and the oiling was improved through revisions to the crankcases, connecting rods, and pistons.

Larger Crankpin and Bearing

To handle the added power supplied by the new top end, a new, larger-diameter crankpin was introduced. The 1940 crankpin was given a 1 1/4-inch-diameter bearing surface (1/8 inch larger than before). It is the same length as the previous crankpin, retains the oil hole and passage from the end to the bearing surface, and tapers at each end from 1 1/8 inches to 1 inch, but now it "steps down" suddenly from the outboard ends of the bearing surface to the start of the taper, so that the new crankpin could be used with the old flywheels. The new, matching main bearing is 1/8 inch larger in diameter and has 54 rollers (instead of 42) for a substantial increase in strength. Both crankpin and bearing remained in use through the end of the Knucklehead line in 1947.

New lapping machinery at the factory was put to good use for 1940 production by line lapping the pinion and sprocket shaft races to ensure perfect sizing and perfect alignment. To make line lapping possible, new bearing races were introduced that did not have the steel plate formerly used with each race. After the crankcases were bolted together and line bored, the new bushings were installed and lapped together. The crankpin and roller bearings were also lapped to "glass smoothness." The result? Smoother, quieter, longer lasting motors.

Crankcase Oil Control

Because the flywheels spin clockwise, when viewed from the right side of the engine, much more oil is slung off them onto the walls of the rear cylinder than onto the front cylinder. To block the bulk of this spray, the 1936–1939 motors had a half baffle covering the rear of the rear cylinder opening. The front cylinder opening had a full baffle to increase vacuum below the piston, with the hope that the vacuum would draw in enough air-oil mist to lubricate the cylinder. This arrangement had worked fairly well—the extra oil on the rear cylinder tending to carry away heat, compensating somewhat for their lack of direct cooling air—but Harley-Davidson decided it could do better, so the company gave a new system a try on the 1939 side-valve Big Twins.

On the 1939 side-valves, the baffles at both cylinder openings were removed, the positions of the connecting rods were reversed (the female rod was moved to the rear cylinder position and the male rod to the front), and half of the slot around the big end of the female rod was closed. Why? The new rod positions tended to sling much less oil on the rear cylinder, so the rear baffle wasn't needed to block direct oil spray. And the half-filled slot on the female rod's big end tended to catch oil and throw it on the front cylinder, so the front baffle plates were no longer needed.

The revised female rod slung enough oil on the front cylinder that Harley-Davidson found it necessary to fit the front piston with an oil-control ring for the first time, so now both front and rear pistons had the same ring configuration: two compression rings and one oil-control. Side benefits were more consistent vacuum throughout the lower end and less oil mist, easing the burden of the crankcase breather valve and oil separator. This system worked so well that Harley-Davidson introduced it to the OHV Big Twins for 1940, and the same basic system is still in use on Harley-Davidson Big twins today.

The new system for the Knucklehead required new left and right crankcases and front and rear connecting rods. The 1940 crankcases are similar to the previous case, but the baffle plates and steel plates for the sprocket- and pinion-shaft bearing races were omitted and the casting number and date plate were moved to inside the case. The left case bears the new casting number 112-406, and the right case bears casting number 112-404. These cases (set up for the new rod positions and bearing races, but still designed for 8-1/8-inch-diameter flywheels) are correct for 1940 only. The new rods bear casting number 40A 706 (male) and 40A 705 (female) and were good enough to remain in service through the early 1970s.

The final lower-end update for 1940 was to the pinion-shaft assembly. The spacer that had been in between the left side of the oil-pump gear and the bearing was replaced for 1940 by a seal ring. Also, a spacer was added between the right side of the pump gear and the spring that fills the space between the pump gear and the pinion gear. Both these changes were used thorough the end of Knucklehead production in 1947.

Transmission and Clutch

For 1940, the standard transmission was once again the constant-mesh four speed because 1939's four-speed transmission with sliding second gear had not been popular among solo riders. Shifting between the constant-mesh first gear and sliding second required more deliberate effort than between the constant-mesh first and second of the pre- and post-1939 four speeds. Perhaps worse than the slower shifting, neutral was in an odd position on the 1939 transmission—between second and third—making it necessary to shift through second when shifting from first to neutral or from neutral to first.

Although it meant swallowing a bit of pride and a lot of design effort, switching back to the constant-mesh four speed was the right thing to do. It was the standard transmission through the end of Knucklehead production in 1947. Returning with the four speed was the 1-N-2-3-4 (front to rear) shifter gate. This gate is correct through 1946.

The sliding gear transmissions were more popular with police and commercial users, however, so the three-speed and three-speed-with-reverse transmissions with sliding-gear first were optional again for 1940-and-later Knuckleheads.

Front brake drums were cast nickel-iron (rather than being stamped steel) with an integral stiffening ring for 1940. The brake shackle was slightly updated, as well. The new shackle has only one grease fitting, at the backing-plate end of the shackle. The fitting for the fork end of the shackle was moved to the fork-end mounting stud, pointing out to the left, as shown. The fender-top trim for 1940 included a chevron and stripes for the front fender. The chevron is visible just ahead of the fender light.

All the 1940 transmissions were updated with the breather on the transmission case (rather than on the starter cover) for 1940. This change required a new transmission case with a boss for the transmission vent plug, and a new starter cover with an undrilled vent boss. The case and cover were otherwise unchanged.

To reduce chatter and to take up slack to prevent rattle, four-slotted spring keys were added to each lined clutch disc. These spring keys fit into the keyways of the clutch ring.

Frame

Only one significant change was made to the frame for 1940: a horizontal toolbox bracket is riveted to the frame's toolbox strap. Starting in 1941, the bracket became a separate piece.

The rear fender of the Pierces' 1940 Knucklehead shows the three fender-top trim pieces that were included in the Deluxe Solo Group, an accessory rear fender tip, and an aftermarket bumper. The saddlebags appear to be aftermarket, too.

Front Brakes

Front brakes were further refined for 1940. The flimsy stamped front brake drum was at last replaced by a cast, nickel-iron drum with an integral stiffening ring to reduce vibration and chatter caused by flexing of the drum. The stiffer drum allows use of a new brake-shoe operating shaft that is 9/32 inch narrower. It also made possible smoother, more uniform grinding of the braking surface for even smoother braking action. Although the front brake was still next to worthless, the 1940 changes made it as good as it would ever get. This drum was used on all spring-fork civilian Big Twins from 1940 through 1949. Interestingly, the Empire Electric Brake Company began marketing the Magdraulic Electric Brake for H-Ds, promising increased stopping power with "The light touch of a Woman's Hand!" All for $22, according to an ad in the April 1940 The Motorcyclist.

Front-brake shackles and studs received minor updates to make maintenance easier. The fork-end grease fitting was omitted on the shackle. Replacing it was a grease fitting on the new nut that secured the shackle to the fork stud. The grease fitting extended to the left from the end of the nut for unrestricted access. Grease pumped through the fitting was channeled through the nut and along a flat ground into the stud's shaft to grease the shackle. The new shackle and stud are correct for 1940–1947.

Saddles

Also updated for 1940 were the standard and deluxe solo saddles. The standard saddle is like the previous saddle, except that the leather covering was changed to tan, smooth-grained cowhide (rather than horsehide) and the pan was made with vent holes. This saddle is correct for 1940–1946.

The 1940 deluxe solo seat was covered in cowhide (again, rather than horsehide) and was given a restyled valance. This saddle was fitted with a short, one-piece leather valance (replacing a longer, three-piece valance). The 1940 valance was made of "walrus grain" leather, to which several jeweled pieces were attached. The valance is fringed, and the fringes grow gradually longer from the sides to the back. The seat was available in tan or black leather—and only for 1940.

Minor Updates

In addition to the major changes already described, the 1940 Knucklehead came with many minor improvements that deserve only brief mention. The forks were heat treated. The top of the oil tank has a raised, vertical rim but lacks the embossed pattern of the previous oil tank. The patent decal is applied to only the left side of the oil tank. The center reinforcement rib on the inner primary cover was lengthened, and a forward-facing bulge was added near the top of the rib. The rear chain guard has its front section spot-welded (rather

They're smiling a bit too broadly to be just watching birds. My guess is that the road they are on ends at Wisconsin's only nudist colony. Binoculars in hand, the young lady on the lightweight 45 takes a closer look. The couple on the powerful "big-port" 61 smile coyly and look but are already planning their get-away from the naked and vengeful posse that will surely follow. The 61 is outfitted with the top-of-the-line Deluxe Solo Group, which added $46 to the $410 cost of the basic machine. Deluxe items shown include the air cleaner, chevron front-fender trim, fender lamp, and chrome-plated instrument panel, wheel rims, handlebar, and relay cover. The spotlamps were accessories available outside the Deluxe group. Note that this bike has the early, sand-cast gear cover. *Copyright Harley-Davidson Michigan, Inc.*

than riveted) to the rear section. The base for the cutout relay was revised to move the relay slightly to make room for the accessory chrome exhaust-pipe covers that had been introduced in 1939. Finally, the brake-side flange of the interchangeable star hub was made of forged steel and its inner surface was redesigned to omit the "step" that had been on earlier hubs. All of these updated parts are correct for 1940–1947.

1940 Production

As the U.S. economy improved, more people had the money to spend on motorcycles. Harley-Davidson's sales rose 26 percent overall to a total of 10,461, the highest total since

1937. Knucklehead sales rose almost 40 percent, to 4,069. Of this total, 3,893 were ELs and 176 were ESs. Most significantly, the 61 OHV—the most expensive model in the line-up—was also the best selling for the first time ever.

Window to the World, 1941

FDR saw the United States' entry into the war as inevitable, so the preparations continued at full throttle. In January, FDR asked for a defense budget of $10.8 billion. In March, Congress passed the Lend-Lease Act, empowering the president to "lend" arms and equipment to the Allies.

In June, U.S. Army troops were sent in to break up a strike, so that production of new warplanes was not interrupted.

The most obvious changes for 1941 were the addition of stainless trim strips fore and aft of the tank badge and the new, "rocket-fin" muffler and exhaust Y-pipe (the pair replacing the fishtail muffler with integral pipe). Other more-subtle changes include a steering-head angle increased to 29 degrees to help stabilize the 16-inch tires, main battery ground attached to a tab on the frame (rather than to the oil line), a new oil pump with centrifugally controlled bypass, and a redesigned brake hand lever. This 1941 Knucklehead is owned by the Trev Deeley Motorcycle Museum in suburban Vancouver, British Columbia. It is a very nice machine, but has a few incorrect bits, including the 1955-and-later deluxe solo saddle and the chrome-plated exhaust pipes (although the chrome header-pipe covers shown were available) and fork springs. The patent decal shown on the right side of the oil tank should be only on the left side of the tank.

Hitler, flush with confidence over the successes of his armies, launched the invasion of Russia.

In September, the *USS Greer* was attacked by a German U-boat, and FDR ordered U.S. forces to attack on sight any Axis vessels in U.S. waters. Taxes were sharply increased to raise money for the defense buildup.

In October, the hawkish General Hideki Tojo took over control of the Japanese government. In November, the U.S. ambassador to Japan warned of an imminent attack on the U.S. military, but the warnings went unheeded. In early December, FDR forwarded a personal appeal for peace to Emperor Hirohito. On December 7, well, you know what happened. Pearl Harbor. And the end of civilian motorcycle production for the duration.

The 1941 Knucklehead

The OHV Big Twin model line expanded in 1941 to include four models, the high-compression 41EL and 41FL Special Sport Solos and the medium-compression 41ES and 42FS twins with sidecar gearing. The new F-series machines were identical to the E-series, except that the F series were fitted with a 74-ci version of the OHV engine.

The EL and ES models were listed at a retail price of $425 ($5 less than in 1940), the FL and FS models at $465. All models had to be ordered with one of the option groups, at additional cost. The 5.00x16-inch tires that had been optional in 1940 were standard for 1941 (except when the Standard Group for sidecars was ordered); the 4.00x18-inch tires were optional for no extra cost.

For 1941, the Utility Solo Group and Sport Solo Group were unchanged. The Deluxe Solo Group included a front safety guard, steering damper, jiffy stand, air cleaner, ride control, trip odometer, fender light, deluxe saddlebags, chrome saddlebag plates with jewels, deluxe solo saddle, colored shift ball, 5.00x16-inch tires, and Chrome Group (chrome-plated rims, handlebars, headlight, instrument panel, taillight housing, relay cover, exhaust-pipe covers, license frame, and top fender ornament).

The 1941 Knuckleheads were available in six standard colors: Brilliant Black, Skyway Blue, Flight Red, Cruiser Green, or Police Silver (police only).

Styling Changes

Styling for 1941 was largely unchanged from that of 1940, the major exceptions being the addition of trim strips to the gas tanks, a restyled speedometer, and a redesigned muffler. In addition, the taillight cover was painted gloss black (rather than the color of the tanks and fenders).

New Tank Trim

The new stainless steel gas-tank trim strips extend horizontally on the centerline of the gas tanks, fore and aft of the same chrome-plated gas-tank emblems that had been introduced in 1940. The result is that, "The stainless steel strips on the tanks blend the front and rear of the motorcycle in one pleasing sweep and add emphasis to the beautiful nameplates," according to the September 1940 *The Enthusiast*. The tank strips replace the pinstripes used on the gas tanks in 1940 and are correct on 1941–1946 Knuckleheads.

"Airplane-style" Speedometer

After five years with the "white-face" style of speedometer, a restyled speedometer was released for 1941 that was influenced by the modern instrumentation in the prominent high-performance aircraft of the day. This new face is difficult to describe; see the photos of it in this chapter. Overall, the face is two-tone, black and silver, in a bull's-eye pattern.

The speedometer's glass is convex, to allow clearance for the thicker pointer, the bezel is chrome plated, and the Harley-Davidson bar and shield is printed in silver at the aft end of the speedometer face. As the September 1940 issue of *The Enthusiast* boasted, "Even the sleek ships that dart through the skies don't have any smarter-looking dials than this one." This speedometer is correct for 1941–1946.

"Rocket-Fin" Muffler

Like the "white-face" speedometer, the fishtail muffler had been carried over essentially unchanged from 1936 through 1940, and the both had definitely begun to look dated on the restyled 1940 machines. For 1941, the Knucklehead's muffler was completely redesigned for a more modern, "Buck Rogers" appearance, with a stylish rocket fin replacing the fishtail of the old-style muffler.

The new muffler is 3 1/4 inches in diameter, much larger than the previous muffler, and was redesigned internally. This muffler departed from standard design practice of the day by not using any steel wool or other internal packing to absorb sound. Instead, it used a resonating chamber to attenuate the exhaust note. The new design had two practical benefits: it didn't grow louder over time because there was no packing to burn up or blow out, and it reduced back pressure for better engine performance. Even without packing, the new muffler was quieter than the old muffler and had a lower, mellower tone. This muffler is correct for 1941–1949 Big Twins. Standard finish was black.

The 1941-and-later muffler lacks the collector pipe that is attached to the front of the 1936–1940 muffler, so a new, separate exhaust pipe was introduced to connect the front and rear headers to the muffler. Because of its shape, the new pipe is called the Y-pipe. This pipe was used on all 1941–1947 Knuckleheads. Like the rest of the exhaust, the Y-pipe is painted black.

Big-Inch Knuckle: The FL

Being the quintessential American motorcycle company, Harley-Davidson eventually came around to raising displacement of the Knucklehead to create a new flagship Big Twin, the 74-cubic-inch Series. Except for its motor, the new model was identical to the venerable Series E.

The extra displacement in the new motor was obtained by increasing the bore by 1/8 inch (from 3 5/16 inches to 3 7/16 inches) and the stroke by 15/32 inch (from 3 1/2 inches to 3 31/32 inches). To obtain these new dimensions, the 74s used new cylinders. The result of the displacement increase was about 5 extra horsepower. To handle the extra power, the lower end and clutch were redesigned for greater strength.

The longer stroke of the 74 made it necessary to use larger-diameter flywheels. The flywheels were made 3/8 inch larger in diameter than the previous flywheel (8 1/2 inches versus 8 1/8 inches) and 4 pounds heavier. In the interest of parts commonality, the 61 engine also used the larger flywheels. Flywheels for the 61 retain the same crankpin-hole dimensions that were used on the previous flywheels (tapering from 1 1/8 inches to 1 inch) so that the crankpin was not changed. Flywheels for the 74 are the same as the 61 flywheels, except that the 74's crankpin holes are placed farther out for the longer stroke and taper from 1 1/4 inches to 1 1/8 inches for the 74's beefier crankpin. These flywheels were used through the end of the Knucklehead line in 1947.

The larger flywheels for 1941 would have been too tight a fit in the existing crankcases, so revised cases were fitted for 1941. The left crankcase was substantially revised, with the top two reinforcement ribs extending up to the cylinder bases and the flywheel cavity increased in size for the 8-1/2-inch flywheels. Except for the larger cavity for the new flywheels, the right case was unchanged. Both cases were used from 1941 through 1947.

The stronger crankpin for the 74 OHV has a cylindrical bearing surface that tapers at each outboard end without a "step" to a threaded end (like the 1936–39 61 crankpin), the larger diameter bearing surface of the 1940–1947 61 crankpin (1.249 inches versus 1.124 inches), and a new taper, from 1 1/4 inches to 1 1/8 inches. It has the same overall length (3.85 inches) as both previous crankpins. This crankpin was used for 1941–1947.

New Clutch

Although the clutch used on the 1936–1940 61s was plenty stout for the added power of the new 74, it displayed a nagging tendency to stick and drag as the many small splines in the hub and notches on the clutch plates wore with use. Harley engineers cured these problems forever with an all-new clutch for 1941.

New Components

The redesigned clutch drum was an all-new part that is larger in diameter than the previous drum and has six keys riveted on the inside of the drum, replacing the 30 keys milled into the inside ring of the previous clutch. These keys mate with notches on the clutch's new plain steel discs. This clutch drum was used without change for 1941–1947.

The 1941 hub was also an all-new part. It is larger in diameter than the previous hub and mates to the clutch's friction plates by a new, more-direct method. The new hub has three long studs (threaded at both ends) and seven long pins (threaded at one end). The new lined discs have 10 matching holes and slide over the studs and pins to mate them solidly to the hub. Ten new clutch springs are used, one on each stud and pin, outboard of the new releasing disc, and the springs are retained by the clutch pressure plate. Nuts threaded onto the ends of the three studs fasten the pressure plate. The outer diameter of the hub is filled with two staggered rows of ball bearings that form the bearing on which the clutch drum freely revolves when the clutch is disengaged. Each row has

For 1941 the speedometer was given a facelift to the "airplane-style" shown. This particular speedometer is the one supplied when the Utility Group was ordered and lacks the trip odometer. When the Sport or Deluxe Solo Group was ordered, a speedometer with a trip odometer was fitted. The upgrade speedometer was just like the one shown except that it had a trip odometer window just aft of the pointer pivot that displayed three digits (two for miles in black on a white background, and one for tenth miles in red on a white background) and the main odometer displayed only five digits, all for miles and none for tenth miles.

18 ball bearings (7/32 inch in diameter). This clutch hub was used without change for 1941–1947.

The 1941 clutch disc pack consisted of a releasing disc, a sprung disc with an asbestos lining on one side and 10 holes for the studs and pins on the hub, three plain steel discs with notches on their outside diameter to mate with the keys on the clutch drum and two spring-loaded balls on each steel disc to reduce looseness and rattling, and three steel discs with asbestos linings on both sides and 10 holes

for the studs and pins on the hub. This disc pack would be used without change for 1941–1947.

Clutch Operation

In operation, the new clutch was much different from the previous unit. On the new clutch, the drum transfers power to the plain steel discs. When the clutch is engaged, spring pressure clamps the plain discs to the lined discs, and the lined discs transfer the power to the clutch hub through the 10 pins on the hub. Overall, the new clutch provides seven total friction surfaces (versus five on the 1940 clutch) with a total of 121 square inches of friction area for an increase of 48 square inches or 65 percent. The new clutch was so effective that it was used almost without change through the end of Knucklehead production in 1947 and on to the Panhead and Shovelhead series of engines that followed.

Revised Clutch Pedal and Bracket

Clutch pedals are subjected to constant use when a bike is ridden in traffic, and the Knucklehead's pedal-pivot bushings were found to wear quickly under such use. For 1941, the problem was fixed through the introduction of a revised clutch pedal on a revised pedal bracket. The clutch pedal has a longer pivot shaft, and the stud for the clutch-rod end is also longer. The pedal's longer shaft inserts through a much longer boss on the revised pedal bracket, and this boss is fitted with two bushings and a grease fitting that provide twice the bearing surface and make for easy lubrication, resulting in much smoother, more durable clutch-pedal action. The bracket and pedal were Parkerized. This bracket is correct for 1941–1944, and the pedal is correct for 1941 through mid-1946.

Carburetors and Intake Manifolds

Because the 1-5/16-inch venturi on the Linkert M-25 had proved to be excessively large on the 1940 61, it was replaced

A new clutch was introduced on all the Harley-Davidson Big Twins for 1941, to handle the extra power of the 74 OHV. It was much stronger, less prone to chatter, and cheaper to produce than the earlier clutch, and it would be used almost without change on all subsequent Harley-Davidson Big Twins into the early 1980s. *Copyright Harley-Davidson Michigan, Inc.*

on 1941 61s by the Linkert M-35 1-1/2-inch carb with a 1-1/8-inch venturi. The new carb cured problems with low-rpm operation, so it was carried over and fitted to all 61s through 1947.

The M-25 was used on the early 74s but was soon replaced by the Linkert M-75, which was also a 1 1/2-inch carb with a 1 5/16-inch venturi. The M-75 carb was used through the end of 1941 production, but was then replaced for the following years by the same smaller-venturi M-35 used on the 61s.

In hot climates or in heavy-duty low-speed use, the OHVs were prone to vapor lock and percolation because the gas in the carburetor would heat up excessively. To fix the problem, the manifold's carburetor pipe was lengthened to space the carburetor farther away from the engine's heat.

Centrifugal-Bypass Oil Pump

For 1941, Harley introduced a new oil pump to fix a long-standing problem on the OHVs—how to properly regulate oil-pump output across the rpm range. To explain the root of the problem, we have to look back to model year 1939. On that year's Knuckleheads a new, larger-diameter drive gear for the oil pump was added to the pinion shaft and a new, smaller-diameter gear was added to the oil pump's driveshaft, effectively "gearing up" the oil-pump drive so that the pump spins almost twice as fast for higher oil pressure and greater flow. Unfortunately, the result was over-oiling at low rpm. Later that year, a lighter bypass spring was introduced to help control the overoiling by opening the bypass channel at 4–6 psi, bleeding off the excess oil. The lighter spring reduced the severity of the overoiling problem, but it was really just an expedient fix that also limited available oil pressure and flow at high rpm. Hardly desirable.

The solution for 1941 was both elegant and effective—a new bypass valve controlled by a centrifugal governor that gradually increases oil flow to the engine as rpm rises. At low rpm, the valve is open, venting most of the oil pump's output to the gear case. At high rpm, the valve is closed, sending all of the oil flow to the engine. The new valve gave the 1941 OHVs optimum oiling at all rpm. The pump worked so well, it was used through the end of the Knucklehead line in 1947. The pump is painted silver.

Frame

To avoid the handling problems associated with use of the now-standard 16-inch tires and a 28-degree neck angle, Harley-Davidson "bumped" the early-1941 frames at the factory, bending them for a 29-degree neck angle. Later frames were given a revised steering-head forging designed for the 29-degree neck angle. Both 1941 frames also came with two other updates: the toolbox bracket was no longer riveted to the frame's toolbox strap, and the battery was grounded on the frame, instead of on the oil line.

7-Inch Air Cleaner

Feeding air to the 1941 carburetors is a new, larger air cleaner. The new air cleaner is superficially similar to the previous air cleaner assembly—the cover fastens to the backing plate with four J-slots, has the bar and shield stamped on the flat surface in the center, and has a data plate riveted to the edge—but is 7 inches in diameter, rather than 6 inches. The backing plate was revised so that the filter's mesh and support are removable as a unit from the backing plate, to make changing or cleaning the air filter easier. The backing plate was Parkerized, and the cover was chrome plated. This air cleaner is correct for 1941–1947 (except that the 1943–1946 covers were painted black).

Small Changes

Many other subtle changes were made to smaller components for 1941. New, "positive-grip" brake hand levers and brackets replaced the old-style "spoon-tip" levers. These levers were die-cast aluminum and were polished for 1941–1942 and for mid-1946 through 1947. (Black-painted steel levers of the same design were used for 1943 through early 1946.) The front-brake backing plate was given a revised anchor with a threaded, 5/16-inch hole for the new-style cable adjusting screw.

A new primary cover was fitted that is 1/2 inch deeper (3 1/4 inches versus 2 3/4 inches) to allow clearance for the 1941-and-later clutch assembly. This primary cover is correct for 1941–1947.

The front rocker housing was revised to have thicker metal in the area around the intake pushrod hole, and the boss around the motor side of the exhaust rocker shaft hole was lengthened to eliminate the need for the adapter sleeve introduced in 1938. This housing is stamped with the new casting number 7049-41.

The front safety guard was revised to allow more cornering clearance. The lower mounts are longer, and the lower bends begin immediately outboard of the lower mounts. From a frontal view, the lower curves are not symmetrical with the upper curves. This guard is correct for 1941–1947.

The deluxe solo seat was revised to again have a three-piece leather skirt with shorter rear skirt and longer side skirts. Each side skirt carries a faceted jewel trim piece near the front of each skirt. The seat is covered in tan or black cowhide.

To allow clearance between the starter-crank arm and the larger-diameter muffler, the starter arm's dogleg bend starts about a quarter of the way up (rather than halfway up) the arm. This crank arm is correct for 1941–1947.

Piston rings were oxide-coated to reduce scuffing and formation of ridges in the cylinder.

The gearshift lever was cyanide-hardened to prevent the shifter gate from cutting into the lever.

A heavier clamping ring was used on the horn to prevent distortion of the diaphragm at high speeds. The horn's tone is slightly lower.

The oil-pressure switch's diaphragm was made of DuPont "Fairprene" for longer service.

The valve stem of the gas shut-off valve was redesigned to give a 1.0-gallon reserve gas supply—1/4 gallon more than before.

The transmission mainshaft nut was redesigned to provide more contact area on the washer, reducing the tendency

ABOVE AND NEXT: The little Knucklehead that could have been. This experimental 45-ci OHV was developed and tested in tandem with the 74 OHV in the late 1930s. It was well-liked by testers but was doomed when a production analysis predicted it would be as expensive to produce as the side-valve 74. Owner Carman Brown reports that the bike is a pocket rocket, able to easily light up the rear tire when ridden hard. The 1941 styling is appropriate because like the 74 OHV, it probably would have been ready for production in 1941 had the project not been canceled.

for the washer to crack. The transmission mainshaft thrust bearings were redesigned for greater thrust strength and were fitted with shields on both sides to keep out foreign matter.

1941 Production

Much of the total Harley-Davidson production for 1941 was for the military. Yet Harley-Davidson still had the capacity to produce a record number of OHV Big Twins for the civilian market—5,149 in all. Of this total, 2,280 were ELs, 261 were ESs, 2,452 were FLs, and 156 were FSs. Then, as now, American riders can never resist bigger engines and more power: the 74 OHVs outsold the 61s 2,608 to 2,541— despite this prediction in the September 1940 issue of *The Enthusiast*: ". . . a limited number of 74 OHV Harley-Davidsons will be produced. However, as I have said, the number will be limited and production will not be nearly as extensive as on the other models."

Window to the World, 1942

By the time the 1942 models began rolling off the line in the early fall of 1941, America was perilously close to entering the war. American factories were churning out planes, tanks, guns, and other military equipment to the exclusion of almost

everything else. And so was Harley-Davidson. With fat contracts to build bikes for United States and Allied forces, and increasing shortages of steel, copper, iron, and aluminum, Harley-Davidson only promised each dealer one new bike for the year. Then came December 7. On January 1, all production of civilian cars, trucks, and motorcycles was halted.

Initially, U.S. troops were steadily forced back all around the Pacific theater of war. In January, Manila fell and American and Philippine forces withdrew to the Bataan Peninsula. They surrendered there in April, and the Bataan Death March began.

In February, FDR ordered internment for all Japanese-Americans on the West Coast. More than 100,000 people were moved inland to internment camps in the following months. On the seventh, Harley-Davidson president Walter Davidson Sr. died. William H. Davidson took his uncle's place at the head of the company.

In June, the United States won its first major victory over the Japanese, in the Battle of Midway. The then-unknown Maj. Gen. Dwight D. Eisenhower was named commander of U.S. forces in Europe. And $42.8 billion was appropriated for the war effort that year—reportedly, more than the entire cost of World War I.

In August, the U.S. Army Air Forces began bombing raids on occupied Europe from bases in England

In December, gasoline rationing took effect nationwide. Fuel-efficient motorcycles once again appealed to the masses. Unfortunately, only used machines were available.

The 1942 Knucklehead

The OHV Big Twin model line for 1942 included the high-compression 42EL and 42FL Special Sport Solos and the medium-compression 42E and 42F twins. The 61s were listed at a retail price of $425, the 74s at $465—both prices the same as the previous year's. All models had to be ordered with one of the option groups, at additional cost.

For 1942, the same option groups were offered again. The Utility Solo Group and the Utility Group (for sidecar machines) were unchanged.

The mid-level option package was the Sport Solo Group, which included a front safety guard, steering damper, jiffy stand, air cleaner, trip odometer, fender light, chrome rims, chrome exhaust-pipe covers, colored shift ball, and 5.00x16-inch tires.

The top option package was the Deluxe Solo Group. This group included a chrome-plated front safety guard, steering damper, jiffy stand, air cleaner, ride control, trip odometer, fender light, deluxe saddlebags, set of jewels for saddlebags, deluxe solo saddle, colored shift ball, 5.00x16-inch tires, Chrome Group (chrome-plated rims, handlebars, headlamp, instrument panel, taillight housing, relay cover, exhaust-pipe covers, license frame, and top fender ornament), and several new items: chrome fender tips, clutch- and brake-pedal rub-

bers, chrome mirror, and chrome parking lamps. This option package made the Knucklehead flashier than ever—but wartime restrictions soon made it impossible to obtain.

Styling Changes

Styling was unchanged for 1942. Even the available colors were not changed. The lucky few customers who were able to get a 1942 Harley had their choice of Brilliant Black, Skyway Blue, Flight Red, Cruiser Green, or Police Silver (police only).

Parts Changes

Just as with the styling, the mechanical configuration of the 1942 civilian Knuckleheads was carried over essentially unchanged. The few changes that were made are briefly noted here.

For 1942–1947, the 74s were fitted with the same, smaller M-35 Linkert carburetor used by the 61s. The larger M-75 carburetor that had been standard on the later 1941 74s was still available as an option.

Because the fuel filter introduced in 1939 (with the fuel line connected to the bottom of the filter) was so unpopular, a new filter (with the fuel-line connection on the side of the filter) was standard for 1942. The new filter was just like the one used from 1936 to 1938, except that the new filter had tapered-flare-nut fittings instead of the older filter's compression-type fittings, and used straight—rather than cross-hatched—knurling. The gas line from the gas tank to the filter was also revised with a slightly different bend for the new

The Deeley 1941 Knucklehead outside the main warehouse and museum building. Trev Deeley is the Canadian importer for Harley-Davidson motorcycles and maintains one of the best motorcycle museums in North America. Starting in 1941, the redoubtable 61 was joined by a larger OHV stablemate, the 74-ci Models F and FL, created by boring and stroking the 61. Along with the 74 OHV came new, larger flywheels and redesigned crankcases, among other changes. The chrome clutch- and chain-inspection covers shown are not stock for 1941; chrome covers were available through the accessory catalogs. The chrome-plated taillight housing is not correct either. Starting in 1941, standard taillight covers were painted black.

connecting point on the filter's side. This filter and line were standard through the end of the Knucklehead line in 1947.

The front brake's cam-operating lever was slightly revised. The 1942–1947 levers are the same as previous levers, except that they have two holes instead of four on the shank and are no longer stamped with the words "SOLO" and "SC."

On 1942–1947 horns, the bracket is peened to the back rather than attached by a screw.

Rocker housings and the oil lines to them were given with nipple fittings (replacing leaky banjo-type fittings) starting in 1942.

The 1942–1946 boattail taillamp was given new spring clips to fasten the glass lenses to the body. The new clips are held in place by four straight-slot countersunk screws, so the taillight body was drilled for these screws.

Padding on the standard seat was changed to spun latex (replacing sponge rubber) padding.

Finally, a new standard gearshift knob was fitted. The new knob consists of a "squashed sphere"—not quite an oval, but slightly wider than it is tall—and a high, stepped ring that

runs horizontally around the sphere, suggesting the rings around the planet Saturn. This knob is correct for 1942–1947.

Finish Changes

Shortages of aluminum and cowhide resulted in changes to some parts for 1942. Aluminum was used to manufacture silver paint and was strictly rationed even in late-summer 1941 when 1942 production began, so the tappet blocks and oil pump were painted white, instead. They remained white until the restrictions began to be lifted in 1946. And cowhide was needed to make boots for all the men who were being drafted, so the seats for 1942 were covered in horsehide.

Weathering the War

With numerous contracts to fill for military motorcycles, H-D was set up to prosper in 1942, despite the war. Not so the company's dealers. With no new machines or parts to sell and with most of their customers off to war, they would have to be clever to survive.

Knowing the plight of its agents, Harley-Davidson sought to help by including helpful advice in the dealer bulletins. The factory urged small, remote dealers to take war jobs and to invest their start-up money in war bonds so they would be ready with enough money to open their shops again when the war ended.

Many dealers took the advice, becoming police motorcycle officers, soldiers, and shipbuilders. The factory urged dealers to secure as much work on police bikes as possible. In the October 19 dealer bulletin, Harley-Davidson urged its dealers to convince their police chiefs to put motorcycles on their 1943 budgets because, "Then, later, if the War Production Board [WPB] should permit production of police motorcycles, your departments should have funds to purchase them." And Harley-Davidson helped woo these scarce customers by mailing out over 3,000 posters to police chiefs.

Other helpful advice? Of course. In the November 16 dealer newsletter, Harley-Davidson provided an answer to every dealer's most pressing dilemma, namely, "What can I get in the way of an appropriate Christmas gift for my police chief and other good customers?" The answer? An official Harley-Davidson memo holder, a mere $1.15 each with orders of five or more.

In the November 30 issue, dealers were advised to send letters or cards to their police customers to "capitalize on gas rationing and get more service work" by emphasizing how regular service work would minimize their bikes' consumption of scarce fuel. This issue also shared the secret for easy installation of the new hard, plastic handgrips: Soak them in hot water before installation.

The December 14 issue reminded dealers to pester the chiefs yet again, this time to have police motorcycles overhauled during the winter months.

To help secure bikes for their showrooms, Harley-Davidson urged the dealers to "try and buy Harley-Davidsons from the boys going to war!"

These bulletins also provide a look at how tightly controlled the supplies of strategic materials had become. Because rubber was so tightly controlled, seals for the rocker housings became unavailable in April 1942.

By May, Harley-Davidson was urging all dealers to send in ruined pistons so that the company could reclaim material to make replacement pistons. Dealers had to supply proof that they had sent in ruined pistons before they could qualify for replacement pistons. All the pistons sent in were pooled "for the common good of all Harley-Davidson dealers." In September, batteries and exhaust valves were restricted to an exchange basis, too.

1942 Production

Despite the shut down of 1942 production, Harley-Davidson records show that 1,743 OHV Big Twins were built. Of this total, 620 were ELs, 8 were ELAs (special ELs for the U.S. Army), 45 were ELCs (special ELs for the Royal Canadian Army), 164 were ESs, 799 were FLs, and 107 were FSs. Those who bought these bikes were fortunate indeed because no more new machines were made available to average civilians until late 1945.

Window to the War, 1943

Steadily gaining strength based on America's production abilities, the Allies began pushing back the German and Japanese advances that had previously seemed so easy in 1940 and 1941.

In January, FDR, Churchill, and Gen. Charles DeGaulle met at Casablanca to discuss war strategy. Sensing that they would ultimately triumph, the Allies agreed that they would accept nothing less than unconditional surrender from Germany, Italy, and Japan. They also agreed to start a second front against Germany by invading Sicily.

In June, income-tax withholding was instituted to improve government cash flow.

In July, the Allied armies invaded Sicily, and Mussolini resigned.

In September, Allied armies invaded Italy. Five days later, Italy surrendered. On September 18, chief engineer and company cofounder William S. Harley passed away.

By the end of the year, America was truly the "arsenal of democracy." Production of B-24 Liberator bombers topped 500 per month at Ford's Willow Run, Michigan, plant alone. American shipyards cranked out 1,949 ships in 1943, among them were 1,238 Liberty ships. And Harley-Davidson was doing its part, too. In 1943, H-D built more than 27,000 military motorcycles.

The 1943 Knucklehead

In principle, the OHV Big Twin model line for 1943 included the high-compression 43EL and 43FL Special Sport Solos and the medium-compression 43E and 43F twins. In principle because Harley-Davidson could build bikes only on special order for customers who had first received WPB approval, which was very difficult to obtain in 1943. Those bikes that were built were likely available with only the items in the Utility Solo Group—front safety guard, steering damper, jiffy stand, 5.00x16 tires, and black rims.

I could not find a source listing the standard colors for the year. Gray was probably the only option, but other colors may have been left over from 1942 production that were used up on the 1943 models. The only reference to colors for 1943 that I could find was in the September 13, 1943, dealer news bulletin, which stated that colors other than standard were offered on police orders for $5 extra.

The only real changes for 1943 were that use of chrome plating, cadmium plating, and silver paint were virtually eliminated. Nearly everything that had been plated on previous models was Parkerized or painted black for the duration of the war and through at least part of 1946, when restrictions on use of critical war materials were eased. The one notable exception to this rule is that the stainless steel tank strips seem to show up on the photos of wartime bikes. Harley-Davidson must have had enough left over from previous years to carry them through the war year. Some bikes may have been fitted with the earlier, chrome or cad-plated parts if any of those parts were left in inventory at the time the bikes were assembled.

So what would one of these wartime machines have looked like? The tank emblems, oil pump, and tappet blocks were painted white. Pushrod tubes, timing-hole plug, seat-post tube, and almost all screws and bolts were Parkerized. The bezel on the speedometer and around the dash's indicator lights were painted black, as were the ignition switch cover, speedometer-light knob, tankshifter and its gate, the handlebar spirals, gas caps, headlamp rim, horn face, front-brake hand lever, front-fender light cover, air-cleaner cover, covers for the horn and headlight switches, steering damper knob, and gas shutoff knob. The stainless steel fender strips were left off. The floorboards for 1943–1947 were painted black and were fitted with ribbed steel (instead of rubber) mats. The rubber blocks on the kickstart pedal were also omitted.

Just about the only chrome-plated parts left on the machine were the four rocker-shaft "knuckle" nuts. In short, the lucky few who were authorized to buy a new Harley got what most would consider an ugly duckling rather than a graceful swan.

Weathering the War

War continued to be hell for cash-strapped Harley-Davidson dealers in 1943, but the factory was there for the dealers again with more helpful hints in the dealer news bulletins.

Although oil was scarce and rationed, Harley-Davidson motorcycles didn't know it. They leaked just as much as they had during peacetime, so the oil needed to be washed off from time to time with a little Gunk. Cans and glass jars were in short supply, so Harley-Davidson was forced to discontinue selling Gunk in small containers. To solve the problem, the factory suggested that dealers buy Gunk in half or full barrels and recycle their old oil jars by filling them with Gunk for resale to customers.

For those dealers who had planned ahead and had heeded the factory's advice of the previous year to court police

Very little changed for 1942 because preparations for war-time production took up most of the time available to the company's design engineers. And then on December 7, 1941, just as production should have been hitting full stride in a normal year, the Japanese attacked Pearl Harbor. Virtually all civilian motorcycle production was stopped by the end of the year. Note the optional jewels covering the saddlebag mounting screws. *Copyright Harley-Davidson Michigan, Inc.*

business, good news was presented in the July 20 dealer newsletter: "A plan long under consideration has now been approved by the proper WPB officers, and police departments having a vital need for motorcycles will be allotted machines in late August or early September."

Even more good news and advice was offered in the August 16 issue: "War plants eligible for new Harley-Davidsons for guard and police duty!" Dealers were encouraged to visit gunpowder plants, air conditioning factories, gun factories, steel mills, and other essential defense manufacturers to encourage them to apply for WPB approval to purchase motorcycles.

Apparently, the police orders began rolling in, because the September 13 issue stated that police bikes ordered with nonstandard colors were $5 extra—implying, of course, that colors other than gray or silver really were available.

Asserting that more Harley-Davidson commercial motorcycles were "very definitely needed to promote the war effort," the November 1 issue urged dealers to court buyers for such machines. The dealers were told to promote the great potential "savings in rubber, gas, and time" these machines would offer to essential war industries for messengers and to deliver shipments. Once convinced of their obvious need for new Harleys, the bosses of these industries would then petition the WPB to allow Harley to build them. You gotta love circular promotion.

The November 15 issue gave the dealers a little pat on the back by trumpeting the results of the court-your-chief campaign: "137 police departments have qualified for new Harley-Davidsons!" Unfortunately, the bulletin gave no indication of how many bikes were allotted to these police departments or what models they were. However, it did include a "purchase proposal for police motorcycles" to show the dealers the proper way to submit a successful request to the WPB. Soon, even the flimsiest excuse would qualify a police department for new machines.

1943 Production

Harley-Davidson records list only 203 OHVs in their 1943 production of over 29,000 motorcycles. Of the total, 53 were ELs, 103 were Es, 33 were FLs, and 12 were Fs. These machines were available only to the very well connected (famous actor or general's son), and those who could demonstrate a compelling, war-effort-related need for a new motorcycle.

Window to the War, 1944

In January, the United States' march across the Pacific islands continued with the successful invasion of the Marshall Islands.

In late February and early March, the U.S. Eighth Army Air Force intensified the bombing campaign against Germany, in a campaign that would come to be known as "Big Week."

In April and May, U.S. forces continued pushing the Japanese from their island strongholds, successfully invading Kwajalein, Eniwetok, Hollandia, and Wake. In June, the Allies struck their most telling blows to date against the Germans. On the fourth, U.S. forces captured Rome. On the

sixth, Allied forces invaded France with an amphibious landing at Normandy. FDR signed the GI Bill of Rights.

In August, Allied forces captured Brittany, invaded southern France, and liberated Paris.

In September, Allied armies pushed into Germany, truly taking the war to The Fatherland and signaling that the end was near. Unfortunately, the Germans still had a lot of fight left in them.

In October, U.S. forces returned to the Philippines, and the U.S. Navy thrashed the Japanese navy in the Battle of Leyte Gulf.

In November, FDR won his fourth presidential election. Harry S. Truman became vice president. The end grew near for Japan, and Hideki Tojo's military government fell.

In December, German forces began a surprise offensive—the Battle of the Bulge—in the Ardennes. The offensive initially forced back the overconfident Allied armies, but was soon routed. By the time the Germans retreated, almost 77,000 Americans had been killed or wounded.

One of the few things that did change for 1942 was a slight redesign of the taillight. To make it easier to assemble the taillight, the internal clips that held the lenses in place were replaced by spring clips fastened by the four straight-slot, cad-plated, countersunk screws down the longitudinal centerline of the taillight cover, as shown in the photo. The side screws shown are not correct. They should be straight-slotted and Parkerized.

For the next three and a half years, the company spent most of its time on military projects, including the manufacture of military motorcycles for the Allies, such as these WLAs for the U.S. Army. *Copyright Harley-Davidson Michigan, Inc.*

Throughout most of the desperate fighting of 1944, Harley-Davidson motorcycles were there. During the year, The Motor Company continued to contribute, building 16,887 military motorcycles.

The 1944 Knucklehead

According to the 1944 order blank, the OHV Big Twin model line for 1944 included the high-compression 44EL and 44FL Special Sport Solos for $425 and $465, respectively, and the medium-compression 44E and 44F medium-compression twins, also for $425 and $465, respectively. Non-police solo bikes were available with only the items in the Utility Solo Group—front safety guard, steering damper, jiffy stand, 5.00x16 tires, and black rims. The only standard color listed was gray or silver—the factory's option, not the orderer's.

Wartime restrictions once again prevented any significant changes. The only mechanical change was that a small spring was added to each of the clutch hub's long studs. Harley's stocks of rubber tires were depleted, so "S-3" synthetic-rubber tires were fitted. And Linkert's supply of silver paint was used up, so carburetor bodies were painted black and would remain black even after the war.

Weathering the War

As the Allies began to get the upper hand in 1944, the supply situation gradually loosened up at home. Still, the

dealers had to scramble to secure enough business to support themselves. Again, Harley's news bulletins were there to help.

The March 20 issue announced triumphantly, "You can get OHV models on your essential civilian and police orders!"—providing the first proof, besides the notoriously unreliable production figures the company published, that OHV models were really made for civilian use during the war. The article went on to specify that even the top-of-the-line 74 OHV models were available.

The April 17 issue informed dealers that the resins used in paints were now even further restricted, so the factory could no longer guarantee that replacement tanks and fenders would be painted. Primed parts would be substituted, if supplies of paints were exhausted.

Although paint was in short supply, plastic for handgrips apparently was not. The May 1 issue announced that dealers could get all the handgrips they needed, and that these grips would not count against their "parts quota."

As the Allies marched to victory after victory, they naturally captured thousands of prisoners. Many of them ended up in prison camps in the United States and Canada. And all those hapless POWs presented the enterprising Harley dealer with still more opportunity for profit. The June 26 issue claimed, "War prisoner camps present added police problem!" and urged all Harley dealers near the camps to contact the security officials in the camps and police in the area to

Starting in 1942, certain materials became unavailable for use on motorcycles. First, it was silver paint (which contained ground aluminum), so the oil pumps and lifter blocks were painted white, as shown here, when stocks of paint ran out in late 1941. Later, chrome and cadmium became scarce, so pushrod tubes, tank badges, air-cleaner covers, screws, and other parts that would normally be plated were painted or Parkerized. Curiously, the pushrod retainers appear to be plated, rather than Parkerized. Perhaps there were still some plated parts left in the bins when this engine was assembled. The photo also illustrates several features that had been changed earlier: the nipple-type fittings for the oil line to the rocker housings that had changed in 1942 and the "handle" added to the pushrod retainers in 1940. Harley records label this as an advertising photo of a 1944 engine. *Copyright Harley-Davidson Michigan, Inc.*

This left-side view of the 1944 engine shows more examples of the wartime finish changes: Parkerized plumber's nuts on a white-painted manifold and Parkerized timing-hole plug, among others. It also provides a good overall view of engine features that are normally difficult to see on an assembled motorcycle: the extended reinforcing ribs on the crankcase (introduced in 1941), the updated crankcase breather pipe (lower right of photo, introduced in 1939), and the "flat-topped" rocker-shaft brackets (introduced in late 1938). *Copyright Harley-Davidson Michigan, Inc.*

"acquaint them with the procedures to obtain as many Harley-Davidson police motorcycles as their needs make necessary."

As these "tips" to the dealers show, the WPB's process of allocating machines where they were needed most had become a farce by mid-1944 and would only get worse (or better) as the year continued.

The October 9 issue recommended that dealers sell the 74 flatheads to all customers because orders could be filled faster than if 61 or 74 OHVs were ordered.

The October 23 issue suggested that dealers buy special Harley-Davidson pigskin wallets as Christmas gifts for police chiefs and other favored customers. A modest bribe, at $2.10 from the factory.

Although not spoken of in the news bulletins, Harley-Davidson dealers were gifted with a new source of motorcycles to sell in mid-1944. *Shop Dope No.* 233 said, "During the past four months, the Government has sold a large number—possibly 3,000 to 5,000—Army surplus, used Harley-Davidson military-model motorcycles. . . . Included in the motorcycles

already sold are 800 to 900 XA shaft-drive models. . . . A portion of both types of these motorcycles have been purchased by Harley-Davidson dealers."

Showing how loose the regulations had become, the November 20 issue featured a photo of a mine mechanic for the Sentry Coal Company of Madisonville, Kentucky, who shuttled between the company's mines on his new 1944 OHV. The issue also trumpeted that 380 police departments recently received approval to buy new motorcycles.

The November 30 issue presented the news flash that the following police departments received new bikes: Los Angeles got 59; Milwaukee got 21; Portsmouth, Virginia, got 5; Akron got 5; Kansas City, Missouri, got 15; and Waukegan, Illinois, got 1. It was almost beginning to resemble a normal production year.

1944 Production

Eligibility criteria were eased somewhat during 1944, so civilian OHV production more than doubled to 535. Of this total, 116 were ELs, 180 were Es, 172 were FLs, and 67 were Fs.

Window to the War, 1945

By the start of 1945, a swift end to World War II seemed a foregone conclusion. The American and British armies

were building a bridgehead to cross the Rhine, and the Russians were poised to sweep into Germany. And in the Pacific, the U.S. Marines were catching their breath before assaulting the last islands on the way to Japan itself.

In February, U.S. forces captured Manila. One of the epic battles of the war began with the United States' invasion of Iwo Jima. The Japanese defenders on Iwo had spent the previous three years preparing over 800 pillboxes to protect the defenders during the expected invasion. The 21,000 Japanese soldiers on the island had been supplied with over 22 million rounds of ammunition and were ordered to fight to the death. The battle would not end for another month.

In March, U.S. forces crossed the Rhine River, one of the last obstacles on the road to Berlin. In the Pacific, the U.S. Marines gain control of Iwo Jima after an incredibly costly battle.

On April 1, U.S. forces invaded the heavily fortified island of Okinawa. Although the landing went almost unopposed, the Americans soon ran into the fiercely determined Japanese defenders

On April 12, less than one month before the fall of Germany, President Roosevelt died of a cerebral hemorrhage as he posed for a portrait in Warm Springs, Georgia. Harry Truman was sworn in as president that afternoon.

On May 7 the war ended in Europe, when Germany surrendered unconditionally. The war on Japan continued.

In June, the American forces on Okinawa gained control of the island. It was one of the costliest victories of the war, however, with over 49,000 Americans killed or wounded. Only the Japanese home islands remained to conquer.

On July 16, the world entered the nuclear age when the first atomic bomb was detonated in New Mexico.

On August 6, a U.S. B-29 Superfortress dropped an atomic bomb on Hiroshima. The next day, Truman promised a "rain of ruin" if the Japanese did not surrender. They did not answer. On August 8, more than two months after the fighting stopped in Europe, Russia declared war on Japan. The next day, an atomic bomb was dropped on Nagasaki. On August 14, Japan surrendered unconditionally.

On September 2, almost six years after the war began, it officially ended when the formal Japanese surrender was signed on the deck of the battleship USS *Missouri*.

President Truman ordered a full return to consumer production. Back in Milwaukee, Harley-Davidson gladly followed Truman's order and prepared to grab their hard-earned share of postwar prosperity.

The 1945 Knucklehead

The OHV Big Twin model line for 1945 included three versions of each model, the high-compression 45EL

A very rare 1944 FL owned by Adolph Ogar. This bike is even more rare in that it is restored to subdued wartime finish. On the wartime machines, almost all parts that had been chrome or cadmium plated were Parkerized or painted. Their very "plain-ness" gave these machines a certain dignity that their tarted-up siblings lacked. *Sheryl Laws*

A Knucklehead even Gen. George S. Patton would have loved. This experimental twin-Knucklehead powerplant was designed for the Royal Canadian Army to power an experimental light tank. The project was canceled after prototypes had been built.

Although the Knuckleheads were considered too complex and costly for general military service, the U.S. Army bought eight Model ELAs, and the Royal Canadian Army bought 45 ELCs, both in 1942. Several other interesting military Knucklehead experiments were carried out. Among them were the XT three-wheeler project shown and an odd experimental powerplant for a Canadian minitank that used two Knucklehead motors. Both projects were canceled after demonstrators had been built. *Copyright Harley-Davidson Michigan, Inc.*

and 45FL Special Sport Solos for $463.67 and $465.00, respectively, the medium-compression 45E and 45F twins at the same prices as the EL and FL, and the 45ES and 45FS twins with sidecar gearing, again, at the same prices as the EL and FL. One has to wonder why anyone would order the 61 models when they were only $1.33 cheaper than the 74 OHVs.

Interestingly, an additional $4.08 ($2.04 per tire) surcharge was levied on the 74 OHV models for their synthetic tires, raising the base price to $469.08. The cost of these tires was built into the base price for the 61 models. The only standard color available was gray.

These bikes were available with the Utility Solo Group—front safety guard, steering damper, jiffy stand, 5.00x16 tires, and black rims—which cost $14.50 extra or the Utility Group for sidecar or package truck motorcycles (which was the same as the other utility group, minus the jiffy stand) for $12. Beginning in March, this option group also included a tripmeter because the nontripmeter speedometers were no longer available, according to the March 12 dealer news bulletin. The $1.50 extra that Harley-Davidson added for the tripmeter raised the price of the option group to $16.00.

The 1945 OHVs were also available with a new option group, the Special Solo Group, which included a front safety guard, steering damper, ride control, jiffy stand, air cleaner, rear safety guard, trip odometer, mirror, 5.00x16-inch tires, sheepskin saddle cover, solo windshield, and black rims—all for $44.50. Beginning in September, a shock absorber

replaced the ride control in the Special Solo Group and the group price was raised to $55.00, according to the September 9 dealer news bulletin. The shock was also available for order without the group for $15.00. It is not clear whether the bikes built around September 9 were 1945 or 1946 models.

Production of military Harley-Davidsons had begun to slow, so time was available to make a few more mechanical improvements for 1945 than had been made in previous wartime years. The generator drive gear's outside diameter was increased from 1.0 inch to 1.022 inches. The new gear was used through 1947. The spring-ring groove was omitted from the clutch pushrod used from 1945 through 1947. And an Oilite bushing replaced the plain bushing and grease fitting on the 1945–1947 clutch-pedal bracket.

Weathering the War

Victory was at hand in 1945, but the dealers were still fighting a war of their own against shortages of bikes and spare parts—and, of course, government red tape. Once again, however, the dealer news bulletins gave hope that the dealers would survive.

The February 12 issue gave the first indication that parts and accessories would again be available when it announced the reintroduction of Speedster handlebars.

The April 9 issue boasted that 450 police departments were approved for new machines.

Even though the Nazis had already surrendered, the May 21 issue made it clear that "VE-Day has brought no change in production of current Harley-Davidsons!" Furthermore, the company asserted that there would be "no special priority on motorcycles for veterans," and that dealers should be "tactful" in explaining the situation to former GIs.

As the war wound down to its satisfying end, even more new surplus items were offered through the dealers. The June 4 issue announced that Army saddlebags would be available for $12.50 retail per bag.

The July 30 issue informed dealers that buddy seats were once again available for the 61s, which means they were available for all the Big Twins because they all used the same seat.

The August 27 issue proclaimed, "A new era dawns with war's end" and promises a swift resumption of civilian production.

Only a week after the surrender of Japan was signed, the September 10 issue revealed that "effective immediately" a shock absorber for the front forks was included with the new Special Solo Group; the shock was also available separately for $15. The price for the Special Solo Group was raised to $55. The November 12 issue announced the return of black rubber grips to replace the hard-plastic grips mandated by the WPB.

Option groups! Accessories! Rubber grips! Normalcy! Thank the Lord! Thank the Bomb! And FDR, God rest his soul. The hard times really were over!

1945 Production

As a result of eligibility requirements being further relaxed so that just about any police department could qualify, and the end of the war, Harley-Davidson's civilian production tripled to 1,430. Of this total, 398 were ELs, 282 were ESs, 619 were FLs, and 131 were FSs.

Window to the World, 1946

With the war over, life at home slowly returned to normal. FDR's New Deal was replaced by Truman's Fair Deal, as in "every segment of our population, and every individual, has a right to expect from his government a Fair Deal."

But after four years of restrictions on their right to strike and frozen wages, America's workers didn't think they were getting a fair deal. Four-and-a-half million workers struck during the year. Major strikes at GM, U.S. Steel, and in the coal mines resulted in major gains for the workers.

Prices rose rapidly because consumers had more money than ever, after four years of wartime thrift and little to spend the money on because American industry was slow to resume production of consumer goods. After so many years of austerity, people were in the mood to splurge.

As the U.S. military scaled back from 11 million to 1 million, birth rates rose 20 percent, starting the "baby boom."

Overseas, relations between the United States and the Soviet Union degraded into suspicion and hostility as Stalin closed borders, isolating eastern Europe completely from the West.

Justice was meted out to the surviving Nazi leaders at the conclusion of the Nuremburg war-crimes trials. The most prominent Nazi to be tried, Hermann Goering, cheated the noose by biting into a cyanide capsule one hour before he was to hang.

The big news in science was the invention of the computer. At the University of Pennsylvania, the world's first electronic calculator, the Electrical Numerical Integrator and Calculator (ENIAC), was demonstrated. Not quite portable, the new machine used 18,000 vacuum tubes to perform 5,000 steps per second.

With its commitments to the war effort successfully completed, Harley-Davidson eagerly resumed the business they new best, the production of America's best motorcycles.

The 1946 Knucklehead

The OHV Big Twin model line for 1946 included three versions of each model—the high-compression 46EL and 46FL Special Sport Solos for $463.67 and $465.00, respectively, the medium-compression 46E and 46F twins at the same prices as the EL and FL, and the 46ES and 46FS twins with sidecar gearing, again, at the same prices as the EL and FL. Again, the 61 models were only $1.33 cheaper than the 74 OHVs. All prices were the same as the previous year's, and the additional $4.08 ($2.04 per tire) surcharge was still levied on the 74 OHV models for their synthetic tires, raising the base price to $469.08. The cost of these tires was still built into the base price for the 61 models. For 1946, two standard colors were initially available: red or gray.

As in 1945, two option groups were offered, both unchanged. See the discussion that follows for more information on option groups.

The early 1946 machines, built in late 1945 and early 1946, were only slightly dressier than their wartime siblings

Some throwbacks to wartime austerity retained on Engesether's mount are the steel footboard mats and knurled buddy-seat pegs shown, which are thought to have been used into the 1947 model year. The rubber pedal pads may seem out of place with steel footboard mats, but they are not. The February 18, 1946, dealer news bulletin announced that the rubber pedal pads were once again included in the Special Solo Group.

had been because chrome and aluminum were still in short supply. The main difference was that red paint was offered in addition to the wartime gray.

Another color and several equipment options became available as the year progressed. Black rubber grips became available in November 1945, according to the November 12, 1945, dealer news bulletin. Availability of foot-pedal rubbers was announced in the January 21, 1946, news bulletin. On and after February 5, gray was dropped as a color option and was replaced by Skyway Blue, according to the news bulletin of that date.

The February 18 news bulletin heralded the return of aluminized paint, so the color Police Silver was once again available for police models. Aluminized silver paint was probably used again on the tappet blocks and oil pumps after that date, replacing the white paint that had been used during the war. A supplement to the February 18 bulletin also listed new accessories and changes to the Special Solo Group. Added to the group were chrome fender tips, deluxe saddlebags, colored shift ball, and rubber pedal pads, and the price was raised to $75. These new items were also available outside the group.

Apparently, the factory experienced a shortage of four-speed transmissions because the May 27 news bulletin announced that beginning on that date, without notice, an unspecified percentage of nonpolice orders would be shipped with the three-speed in order to maintain production.

Much later in the production run, such niceties as stainless steel for the fender trim and chrome for the pushrod tubes probably became available, and the machines gradually began to look like civilian motorcycles again. Even though many 1946 OHVs were wartime plain, they looked like

Harley's February 18 dealer news bulletin also specified that chrome fender tips, colored shift ball, and deluxe saddlebags were added to the Special Solo Group, so chrome was becoming available enough again by that date for use on frivolous decoration. Based on the fact that chrome was available for fender tips, it is likely that around this time chrome-plated pushrod tubes, tank emblems, air-cleaner covers, shift levers, shifter gates, and horn covers also became available once again. It seems that there was enough stainless steel available during the war that the stainless tank strips were fitted, yet, curiously, the company discontinued the stainless fender strips. These fender strips likely became available again in late 1946. The fringed buddy seat and saddlebags shown are aftermarket items.

sparkling jewels to motorcyclists who had been deprived of new machines for so long. But after the dressier bikes became available once again, the formerly sparkling jewels began to look as plain as they really were. Naturally enough, most of them were soon outfitted with the glossier parts. Original and restored machines with the wartime finishes on their parts are almost never seen.

"Bull-Neck" Frame

Stability problems with the 5.00x16-inch tires had been largely solved when the neck angle was changed from 28 degrees to 29 degrees in 1941. Even so, Harley-Davidson engineers introduced a revised frame for 1947 that had a more massive neck forging with a 30-degree neck angle. The new forging is more massive overall, and the diameter of the neck is larger than the diameter of the neck cup so that less of the cup is visible. Because of its stout construction, the new forging earned the nickname of "bull-neck." This new neck forging is correct for 1946 through mid-1947.

The 30-degree neck angle did give an extra margin of stability and safety, but at the cost of slower, heavier steering—but Harley-Davidson's customers didn't seem to mind. By another degree, the OHV sport bike Harley-Davidson had introduced in 1936 continued its evolution toward its destiny as a heavy, stable touring bike.

Mechanical Updates

After so many years with so few changes, the OHV Big Twin's design was in definite need of some updates, and most of the updates were made as running changes during the production year.

In midyear, a new tab for affixing the spark-control spiral to the frame was added to the lower tank mount on the left front downtube. The separate clamp for the coil was no longer used.

Early in the production run, the forks were given revised spring-rod-ball bushings and a ball-bushing retainer plate. After April 29, according to the October 21, 1946, dealer news bulletin, the inline forks were replaced by "offset" forks that are identical to the inline forks, except that the neck on the offset forks angled back so that it is behind the centerline of the rigid fork legs at the top of the forks. New handlebars were designed with a revised center section for use with offset springer forks. The center hole on the center section is offset to the rear of the two holes for the rigid fork legs. The offset forks and bars were also used in 1947.

About midway through production, the fenders were given wider braces. Still later, the fenders were once again drilled for the stainless steel trim strips that became available after wartime restrictions were lifted. The updated fenders were also used in 1947.

The headlight mount was redesigned to have an integral top horn mount, and the mounts were used again in 1947.

In late 1946, the front rocker housing was slightly revised. The new housing is like the previous housing, except that the bottom surface was milled flat and the mold was revised to thicken the casting in the area around the intake pushrod hole. It was used again for 1947.

Finally, in late 1946 the clutch pedal was recontoured so that the heel pad is offset to the left by about 1/4 inch. It was used again for 1947.

1946 Production

The war was won, the boys were coming home, and most prewar motorcycles were worn out because of the lack of spares during the wartime years. Harley-Davidson was able to sell all the motorcycles it could find raw materials to build. According to the September 1946 *The Enthusiast*, "The demand for new Harley-Davidsons has been so over-whelming that we found it necessary to allot motorcycles to dealers on a quota basis." Despite shortages, production rose to 6,746 OHVs, higher than for any preceding year. Of this total, 2,098 were ELs, 244 were ESs, 3,986 were FLs, and 418 were FSs.

Clearly, the market was still there in postwar America for Harley-Davidson's flagship Big Twin—all the company had to do was figure out how to make enough to satisfy the demand.

As mentioned in previous captions, most of the "civilian-shiny" parts shown here probably were available by the end of the 1946 production year. The plainer, earlier bikes have almost all been updated for a better appearance over the years—and who can blame the owners for having done so?

CHAPTER FOUR

1947

The Last Knucklehead

Optimism. That's the word that summed up the mood of the country for 1947. The economy was booming again. Unemployment was down to 3.9 percent, and the GNP was rising at the rate of 11 percent per year. Farmers were raising bumper crops, yet prices stayed high. The only blight was the high inflation rate of 8.4 percent, fueled by the housing shortage. The last real vestige of wartime shortages of consumer goods, sugar rationing, finally ended midyear, and meat consumption rose to five nights a week for the average American family. Over a million former servicemen entered college on the G.I. Bill and prepared for a more prosperous future.

If anything, the mood was even more jubilant at the Harley-Davidson factory in Milwaukee. After weathering the Great Depression, World War II, and the shortages and rationing that were the war's lingering legacy, the company was stronger than ever. And their OHV Big Twin, the flagship of the world's largest motorcycle fleet, was still the best and most technologically advanced American production motorcycle, 11 years after its introduction. Harley's main rival, Indian, was still peddling flat-heads and was rapidly losing market share to Harley-Davidson's OHV. Despite shortages of materials that had kept Harley-Davidson from meeting demand, 1946 had been the best sales year ever for the OHV; more than 6,000 were sold.

As the 1947 models began rolling off the production line in the fall of 1946, the company was also busy preparing an extensively updated version of the OHV motor that would gain its own fame under the nickname "Panhead." If the Knucklehead was so popular and so technologically far ahead of the competition, why expend the effort to replace it? Because Indian wasn't the real competition anymore—heightened expectations and new machines from overseas were.

When the Knucklehead was introduced, biplanes were still the norm in the U.S. Army Air Corps. By war's end, even sleek, 400-mile-per-hour monoplanes like the P-51 Mustang looked obsolete compared to the jet fighters that were just entering service. By early 1947, jets were the norm, and the even-faster rocket-powered experimental planes were the leading edge.

At the same time, light, fast, sophisticated motorcycles were beginning to flood onto U.S. shores from Great Britain. The young and the reckless who had been the primary market for motorcycles—which in that era included thousands of discharged pilots, sailors, and soldiers who were looking for a new jag to replace the terrifying thrills of combat—were not going to be satisfied for long with Harley's old biplane.

While Harley-Davidson probably could not have guessed how thoroughly the middleweight British machines would come to dominate the U.S. market in the next 10 years, they didn't care because the testosterone-charged dare-devil was no longer the company's intended customer. After all, these customers were fickle, likely to switch to the hottest new machine to come along, whatever the brand. For better or for worse, Harley-Davidson abandoned these riders to the British and staked the company's future on making their motorcycles appeal to a larger segment of society and hooking their customers for life.

Turns out this was a great long-term strategy but a poor short-term tactic because there were more perfor-

Jeff Coffman's bagger probably would have won the "best-dressed machine" award at one of the AMA club events of the day.

After six years without much change, the styling of the Harley-Davidson Big Twins was updated in 1947. The most obvious change was the new, streamlined tank badges. These emblems were penned by famous industrial designer Brooks Stevens. Also updated were the taillight, instrument panel, and speedometer. This nice 1947 FL, owned and restored by Carman Brown, shows a top-of-the-line bike with almost every option, and even some extra chrome that wasn't available on a new machine, such as the exhaust pipes, muffler, and rear safety guard. The saddlebags are aftermarket bags designed to mount to the rear fender rack.

mance oriented customers waiting than Harley-Davidson would ever have guessed. More than 10,000 British motorcycles were sold in 1946, and another 15,000 in 1947.

As we have already seen, Harley-Davidson began trading performance for civility on the Knucklehead during its very first year, and by 1947 the design of the bike had evolved so far away from its sport-bike origins that there was no turning back. So when the company introduced its redesigned engine for 1948, it was one that would help carry the company further down the evolutionary path leading toward the big, reliable cruisers it still builds today.

In the meantime, Harley-Davidson kept its corporate fingers crossed. Barring any unforeseen shortages or a fresh outbreak of war, 1947 looked to be the year the company would cash in.

Window to the World, 1947

Tensions heated up between the United States and the Soviet Union and between the U.S. government and its few dissenting citizens. Bernard Baruch coined a chilling phrase when he implored: "Let us not be deceived. Today we are in the midst of a cold war. Our enemies are to be found abroad and at home." The United States embarked on its policy of "containing" the Soviets. As part of the containment strategy, President Truman requested $17 billion for aid to America's war-ravaged allies and enacted the Marshall Plan to rebuild Europe.

Who were the enemies at home? Like Kilroy was during the war, these enemies were everywhere, especially in government and in the movies. President Truman ordered FBI loyalty checks on federal employees to weed out "Socialists, Communists, and fellow travelers," and the House Un-American Activities Committee investigated the Communist infiltration of Hollywood. Instead of containment, suspected communists in Hollywood were "blacklisted."

The sport of motorcycling was given a black eye as a result of exaggerated publicity of a few instances of inebriated motorcyclists taking liberties in the town of Hollister, California, on July 4. The movie *The Wild One*, starring Marlon Brando, was later based on the incident.

Television continued its takeover of the air waves. The World Series (Dodgers versus Yankees) and a presidential speech (in which President Truman implored Americans to conserve on food so that more could be sent to Europe) were each televised for the first time. Exciting new shows like *Howdy Doody* mesmerized the first of the baby boomers, and the Kraft Television Theater proved the marketing potential of the new medium as sales of Kraft cheese skyrocketed.

Strife between labor and industry continued. Telephone workers and coal miners struck and made major gains before unions were neutered by the provisions of the Employers Rights Act. Henry Ford, perhaps the staunchest opponent of unions, passed away on April 7.

Advancing science, a new "cure" for schizophrenia was announced: the prefrontal lobotomy. Edwin Land invented the Land camera. Admiral Richard Byrd explored Antarctica.

Progress in aviation really took off. Pan American Airways began round-the-world service in the Lockheed

Here's one owner's vision of a custom 1947 Knuckle, mostly in stock form, but with blacked-out chrome on the spirals, air-cleaner cover, and gas caps, and no stainless fender trim. This machine was restored by Elmer Ehnes per owner Jim "Aard" Conklin's specifications.

Constellation *America*. The big one occurred on October 14, when the laconic Capt. Charles E. Yeager—flying the world's most dangerous aircraft despite having broken his ribs in a tumble from a horse—flew the Bell X-1 rocket plane through the "sound barrier" over Muroc Air Force Base to become the first hero of the supersonic age.

Jackie Robinson became the first African-American player to break the "color barrier" in the major leagues when he signed with the Brooklyn Dodgers.

And Harley-Davidson was poised to break through a barrier of its own, the 20,000-sales barrier. Not since 1929, the year of the stock market crash that started the Great Depression, had sales of the company's civilian motorcycles surpassed this mark.

The 1947 Knuckleheads

By 1947, the Knucklehead's major shortcomings had all been ironed out, so most of the changes were limited to restyling to give it a fresh, new, postwar look.

The OHV Big Twin model line for 1947 included the high-compression 47EL and 47FL Special Sport Solos, the medium-compression 47E and 47F solo twins, and the 47ES and 47FS twins with sidecar gearing. The EL, E, and ES models were listed at a retail price of $590 (almost $130 more than in 1946), and the FL, F, and FS models were listed at $605 ($145 more than in 1946). As the listing shows, retail prices had increased over 20 percent for 1947, mostly the result of the high prices Harley-Davidson was forced to pay for aluminum, steel, rubber, and chrome because of the easing of price controls and lingering scarcity. Other manufacturers were forced to raise their prices, too.

Putting the best possible face on the increase, Harley-Davidson called it "moderate," and boasted in the November

The shifter gate for 1947 was restyled to a boxier, more massive design than that used on the 1936–1946 Knuckleheads. The shift pattern was also reversed so that first was at the rear and fourth was at the front, getting the shift lever out of the way of the rider's knee once the bike was shifted into second or higher gear. Note the shift knob, which is the "Saturn" type introduced in 1942, with the raised ring around its belt line. *Copyright Harley-Davidson Michigan, Inc.*

1946 issue of *The Enthusiast* that, "It is only because of the forsight [*sic*; maybe they were still rationing the letter *e* ?] and judgment gained by long experience, plus advanced manufacturing methods, that prices have been kept down to their present level."

All Harley models had to be ordered with one of the option groups, at additional cost. Again for 1947, only two major option groups were offered for solo motorcycles, but for 1947, two version of each were offered—with hydraulic shock absorber and without. The Utility Solo Group included a trip odometer, steering damper, hydraulic shock absorber, front safety guard, jiffy stand, chrome fender lamp, and 5.00x16-inch tires, all for $34.00 ($26.50 with ride control in place of the shock absorber). Sidecar and package-truck machines were fitted with the Utility Group, which came in two versions and included the same items as the Utility Solo Group, minus the jiffy stand—all for $31.50 ($24.00 with ride control in place of the hydraulic shock absorber).

The only upgrade package offered for solo machines was the Special Solo Group. This group included a trip odometer, steering damper, hydraulic shock absorber, front safety guard, jiffy stand, rear safety guard, set of three foot-pedal rubbers, colored shift ball, deluxe saddlebags, 5.00x16-inch tires, chrome fender light, chrome air cleaner, chrome headlamp, pair of chrome fender tips, chrome exhaust-pipe covers, chrome spotlights and fork bracket, and chrome parking lamps—all for $100.00 ($92.50 with ride control in place of the shock absorber).

The 1947 Knuckleheads were available in four standard colors: Brilliant Black, Skyway Blue, Flight Red, or Police Silver (police only).

Styling

For its last year, the Knucklehead was restyled to give it a more-modern, postwar look. The centerpieces of the restyle—new tank emblem, tankshift gate, instrument panel, and restyled speedometer face—were clustered on the tank, but subtle styling changes stretched all the way back to the new taillight.

"Ball-and-Banner" Tank Emblem

The most visible change for 1947 was the new, streamlined "ball-and-banner" tank emblem. This emblem was designed by noted Milwaukee industrial designer Brooks Stevens, who lent his distinctive style to everything from Evinrude outboard motors to the Excalibur car. Incidentally, when Willie G. Davidson, grandson of one of the company's founders and future vice president of styling, graduated from the Art Center College of Design in Los Angeles, he went to work for Stevens before joining Harley-Davidson in 1963.

At the front, the new emblem has a circular chrome rim with a large red ball in the center and a chrome "speed-line" running horizontally across the ball. Trailing the ball is a long chrome-plated banner that tapers slightly before ending in a blunt chisel point. The company name is debossed on the banner, and the letters are painted red.

Unlike all earlier tank emblems and decals, the 1947 emblems do not follow the rakish angle of the tank's side centerline. Rather, the new emblems are placed near the center of the tank's side, but the centerline of the emblem is perfectly horizontal so that it breaks with the overall flow of the bike's lines, which taper toward the rear axle. The new emblem, suspended alone on the expanse of paint on the side

Another decked-out 1947 Knuckle, this one owned by Jeff Coffman of Jeff's American Classics in Dundee, Oregon, and restored by Jeff and his employees, Mark Dencklau and Glenn Weyrauch. This bike, too, has just about every option offered that year, and some items that weren't, including the dual exhaust with the early-style mufflers. The fender-top trim, saddlebags, bumpers, and buddy seat are aftermarket items.

of the gas tank gave a clean—some would say stark—appearance that further emphasized how much the 16-inch tires had bulked up the bike. This style of tank emblem was also used on 1948–1950 Panheads.

Shifter Gate

The new shifter gate for 1947 was a radical departure in style. From a side view, it is flat and perfectly horizontal (not curved), like the tank emblem. It is also longer (stretching forward beyond the front end of the tank) and thicker (because the edge is bent down). This shift gate is chrome plated and was used through 1965 on hand-shift Panheads.

The markings on the top of the gate reflect another change for 1947—the shift pattern was reversed so that first gear is at the rear and fourth gear is at the front for more knee room. Because most riders do most of their riding in high gear, the gearshift lever is almost always in the rearmost position, where it could interfere with the rider's left knee if that person was long of leg or carried a passenger on the optional buddy seat. While the optional buddy seat was quite long and

had an adequate seat area for two, the rider still had to scoot forward a bit so that even an average-size rider's left knee could run afoul of the shifter.

Sliding in the new gate was a revised shift lever. Because the shift lever used from 1937 to 1946 tucked in very close to the gas tank, it was not useable with the 1947 shift gate, so the bend on the shift lever was revised for 1947 to work with the new gate. The new lever was chrome plated. Although it was a one-year-only part on the Knucklehead, it was carried over onto the new Panhead for 1948.

At the transmission end, the revised shift pattern was implemented by rotating the position of the short gearshift lever on the left side of the transmission by 180 degrees. For 1936–1946, the lever was positioned to point nominally upward; for 1947, it was positioned to point nominally downward, reversing the movement of the transmission lever with respect to movement of the tankshift lever, thereby reversing the shift pattern.

Instrument Panel

Perched atop the gas tanks was a new instrument panel that echoed the lines of the tank emblem. At the front, the

Without all the extras, Jeff Coffman's other 1947 Knucklehead is a fairly trim machine. The speedometer and instrument cover were restyled for 1947, the panel to mimic the styling of the tank emblems and the speedometer with italic numerals and a silver center. Note the center of the speedometer. Factory photos show that the black gradually fades to silver at the very center, but every 1947 speedometer I have seen abruptly changes from black to silver, like the one shown here. This style of speedometer was used only for 1947.

instrument panel encircles the round speedometer dial, much like the front of the emblem encircles the red ball. And the rear of the instrument panel tapers gracefully before ending in a blunt chisel point, just as the emblem's banner does. The instrument panel is painted the main color of the tank.

The panel is fastened to the tank by a chrome-plated mounting bolt located just aft of the speedometer. Rather than separate lenses for the two warning lights, the new dash has just one red lens, located just aft of the mounting bolt. The wide, rectangular, red lens covers the generator- and oil-warning lights. The oil light is on the right, and the generator light is on the left. Aft of the lens is the ignition switch. A hole for the police speedometer lock is on the panel's left side, and a slot for the tripmeter reset lever is on the right side. The new hole and slot covers are retained by clips rather than screws. Also for 1947, the gap between the lower edge of the instrument panel and the gas tank was sealed by a rubber molding.

"Black-Face" Speedometer

Nestled in the front of the new instrument panel was a revised "airplane-style" Stewart-Warner speedometer with a restyled face and a new light position, all of which made the speedometer easier to read at night.

The main difference between the 1947 face and the 1941–1946 face is that the new face no longer has the concentric bull's-eye pattern in black and silver. Instead, the new face has a black background that fades to white at its very center. All the features that were formerly silver—the numerals, hash marks, circular pinstripes, bar and shield, and Stewart-Warner face part number—are now white. For ease of reading, the numerals are thicker and are slanted in italic style, and the pointer is painted red, rather than white. This speedometer is correct for 1947 only.

The light for the 1941–1946 speedometers shone through a plastic window on the edge of the back third of the face. Because of this position, it did a good job of illuminating the bar-and-shield logo and the numerals 10 and 20 on the left and 110 and 120 on the right, but left the numerals for normal operating speeds in the dark because they were at the front of the speedometer, at the farthest point on the face from the light.

On the 1947 speedometer, the light window was shifted clockwise so that most of the light shone on the numerals 10 through 60, the speed range most used. The repositioned light made the thicker, white numerals seem to glow against the black background, so the night rider could read his speed precisely.

Revised Gas Tanks

To accommodate the revised pieces attached to it, the gas tanks were revised with new mounts for the new emblems (and the stainless steel strip mounts were deleted), a recessed mounting area on the left tank for the new shift gate, and reshaped dash-mount bases for the restyled dash. These new tanks are correct for 1947–1950.

This close-up of the forks on Coffman's black 1947 shows the hydraulic shock absorber that first became optional in late 1945. It also shows the new-style horn mount that had been introduced in 1946.

This view with the carburetor removed on Mike Golembiewski's 1947 Knucklehead shows how the oil is routed from the top of the gear-case cover to the rocker housings atop each head.

"Tombstone" Taillight

At the rear, a new taillight was fitted to match the other, more angular styling cues introduced for 1947. Instead of tapering gracefully as the 1939–1946 "boattail" taillight did, the 1947 taillight was squared off at the rear. When viewed from the back, the taillight looks like a tall rectangle with a semicircle on top, a profile similar to that of simple tombstones—hence its nickname.

The taillight body was die-cast zinc alloy. The front of the body's top surface has a cast-in lug, to which the license-plate bracket attaches. On the top of the body, just aft of the license-plate bracket, is a window with a frosted-glass lens that allows light from the taillamp to shine through and illuminate the license plate. The tombstone-shaped red rear lens has a molded-in Stimsonite refractor pattern to diffuse the light.

The standard taillamp body, lens retainer, and license-plate bracket are painted black, but these items may have been available in an optional chrome-plated finish later in the year when chrome became more available. This taillight assembly was used on the 1947 Knucklehead and on all the later Panheads through 1954.

More Chrome and Cadmium Plating

"We are doing everything within our power to supply more chrome and there is more of it on our 1947 Harley-Davidsons than there has been for a long time," boasted the September 1946 issue of *The Enthusiast.* And the magazine wasn't lying. Chrome for plating was far more available than it had been since before the war, so the switch back to shiny finishes on the parts that had begun in 1946 was essentially completed by the start of the 1947 season.

Once again, the handlebar switches, ignition-switch cover, horn cover, front-fender light, instrument-cover mounting bolt, gas shut-off knob, gas caps, speedometer bezel, headlamp ring, and many other parts were chrome plated on the basic motorcycle, and chrome-plated optional accessories were offered, including front and rear fender tips, headlamp bucket, exhaust-pipe covers, and parking lamps.

Similarly, cadmium-plated parts were used in many of the same places as on the prewar bikes: kickstarter tube and end pieces, timer cover, seat-post tube, spoke nipples, light-switch knob for the speedometer, and other small parts. And aluminized paint was once again in steady supply, so the oil-pump body and tappet blocks were once again painted silver. Wartime's ugly duckling once again became peacetime's swan.

New Neck Forging

Late in the 1947 production year, the frame's steering-head forging was given another update. The bull-neck forging that had been introduced in 1946 was replaced by a much-slimmer forging. The neck of the new forging is about the same diameter on its upper and lower edges as the neck cups, but tapers to a much smaller diameter in the center section of the neck. This new neck forging was used only for late 1947.

Coffman wanted to keep this machine light and simple of line, so when he and his crew restored it, they left a lot of extra chrome off and even omitted chrome bits that came standard, such as the chrome on the handlebar spiral. He also left off the red paint that highlights the tank emblems. Authentic in every detail? No, but the few changes he made give the bike a very clean look. Note the low-mounted toolbox. Holes on the toolbox strap for 1947 allowed it to be mounted in either the low or high position.

A Knucklehead in Every Barn

A mong the many secrets I unearthed during two visits to the Harley-Davidson archives is a reference to a top-secret sales strategy that allowed Harley-Davidson dealers to exploit the only segment of the youth market that was benefiting from the postwar inflation. The secret untapped market? Farm boys. Yep, farm boys.

Looking back on the economic conditions during 1947, it doesn't take a supply-side economist to appreciate the obvious genius of the plan. The main beneficiaries of the postwar inflation were farmers, who were still intensively farming every square inch of their land for bumper crops, yet were receiving record prices for the crops because the government was buying incredible quantities of produce to ship to war-ravaged Europe. Naturally, some of the new-found wealth trickled down to farm boys across the fruited plain.

In an article titled "$30 Hogs and Your Motorcycle Market" in the March 10, 1947, dealer news bulletin, Harley-Davidson's sales department outlined the new strategy and exhorted its dealers to exploit this untapped youth market because "farm boys really like motorcycles." Better yet, these boys had money because "dad has been liberal with them—has let them raise a calf or two—a hog—or put in a few acres of crop." Even better, "When they make up their mind to buy a new Harley-Davidson, they have the cash to put right down on the line. No extended payments for them."

Harley-Davidson's sales increased over 25 percent in 1947, compared to 1946, and sales of the OHV models, the most expensive in the line-up, almost doubled. Did farm boys make the difference? I'll leave that answer for an upcoming MBA thesis.

This factory photo shows the new speedometer and instrument panel for 1947. Note how the black speedometer face fades to silver at the very center. All 1947 speedometers I have seen change abruptly to silver at the pinstripes just outboard of the odometer windows. Speedometers with the gradual fade may have been only on the machines in the Harley-Davidson photos or on early production machines. Note that the top plate over the handlebar holes is not chrome plated, and that the fork is of the "inline" springer type used through mid-1946, which indicates that the photo is of a prototype machine based on one of the "plain" 1946 machines. *Copyright Harley-Davidson Michigan, Inc.*

Engine

Mechanical modifications for 1947 consisted of subtle refinements, rather than radical change. The 1947 tappet assemblies were fitted with an updated roller with needle bearings (replacing the roller bushing used from 1936 to 1946) for smoother operation and longer wear. Each new tappet roller assembly consists of a roller, a roller race, a roller axle pin, and 25 needle rollers. The new rollers were used again on the tappets for the 1948 Panhead motor.

The other notable engine update for the year was made to the ignition timer assembly. On the 1936–1946 timers, the cable from the advance spiral on the handlebar is attached to a post on the timer strap, which clamped around the timer's base. For 1947, a new base was fitted. The new timer base has an adjustable post sticking straight

With all the items available that year and later, the Knucklehead, which had been designed as an elemental sporting machine, could be transformed into a long-distance hauler.

to the side, to which the cable is attached, providing a more direct, simpler connection. The timer housing was revised with a 13/16-inch notch on its top rim. The new post on the timer base protrudes out to the side of the timer assembly through the slot. The slot allows clearance for the post to slide clockwise (retard) or counterclockwise (advance), and the slot's edges serve as the advance and retard stops. This style of advance mechanism was also carried over to the Panhead in 1948.

As part of the switch to the new timer assembly, a new cut-out relay base was fitted. Relay bases since 1936 had an integral slot that served as the advance and retard stops for the pre-1947 timer assembly. The new relay base for 1947 lacks the slot. A redesigned bracket was used to fix the control coil in place.

The new taillight introduced in 1947 was quickly dubbed the "tombstone" taillight because of its shape. It had an integral license-plate frame, a top window to illuminate the license plate, and a red "Stimsonite" refracting rear lens. The chrome-plated rear lens retainer was optional; the standard retainer was painted black.

Coffman's black 1947 Knucklehead has the "bull-neck" frame introduced in mid-1946 and used through most of 1947 production. Note how heavy the casting is around the lower cup for the steering-head bearing.

Clutch

To simplify assembly at the factory, the 1947 pressure plate and pressure-plate nuts were revised. On the 1941–1946 clutch, the pressure plate was secured by three nuts and lock washers to the three threaded studs that extend out from the clutch hub. For 1947, the pressure plate was redesigned to have a bump along the edge of each stud hole, and the nuts were redesigned to have notches. Each bump mates with a notch in its respective notched nut to prevent the nut from turning, so no lock washers are needed. The new pressure plate and notched nuts were good enough to be carried over to the Panhead series in 1948, then on to the Shovelhead series that followed in 1966, and all the way through the last Shovelheads in 1984.

Seats

With the war over, cowhide was available again. For 1947, the standard solo saddle was covered in black cowhide, replacing the brown horsehide that had been standard since 1942.

The optional deluxe solo seat was restyled for 1947. This seat is covered in black horsehide and has a black plastic

valance that gets gradually wider at the sides and tapers to be very short at the rear. The valance is decorated by a row of small nickel dots along the lower edge of the skirt and has a plastic rosette on each side of the valance. Smaller nickel pieces flank the rosettes, three to the front and one to the rear. This seat was carried over onto the Panhead series for 1948–1954.

1947 production

As the company had hoped it would be, 1947 was the best year for civilian sales since 1929—despite the substantial increase in price. Harley-Davidson's records suggest that it sold 20,115 motorcycles in 1947. Of this total, 11,348 were Knuckleheads, including 4,117 ELs, 237 ESs, 6,893 FLs, and 401 FSs.

While sales of 11,000 Knuckleheads in a single year may not seem all that significant, comparison with sales figures

Brown's 1947 Knucklehead carries the deluxe solo seat that was optional from 1947 to 1954. Whitewall tires were not available on a new machine from Harley-Davidson in 1947, but may have been available from the aftermarket.

from other years shows just how important the OHV Big Twin had become to the company. In its first year, 1936, only 1,700–2,000 Knuckleheads were built, which represented about 20 percent of Harley-Davidson's motorcycle production. In its final year, 1947, Knuckleheads accounted for more than half of Harley-Davidson's sales. In its first four production years, 1936–1939, only about 9,300 Knuckleheads were built, almost 2,000 fewer than were sold in 1947 alone. In fact, almost one third of all Knuckleheads ever built were built in 1947. Even so, demand had not been met. What had once been a temperamental hot-rod for the devil-may-care few had become a workaday mount for motorcycling's equivalent to "the masses."

The Future

Fall of 1947 brought with it the end of the Knucklehead, but a new beginning for H-D. The November 1947 issue of *The Enthusiast* announced the "biggest motorcycle story of the year," the new OHV models that would carry the company into the future.

The big story? An updated top end for the OHV engine, consisting of aluminum cylinder heads, hydraulic valve lifters, redesigned cylinders with internal oil feed and return lines to and from the heads, and a chrome-plated, stamped-steel "pan" cover that completely enclosed the rockers and valves of each head. These updates made the motor smoother, quieter, more oil tight, cooler running, and more maintenance free, but not much lighter or more powerful.

Other than the top end, little else was changed for 1948. Even the styling was almost exactly the same as on the 1947 OHV. The changes that turned the Knucklehead into the Panhead were evolutionary, not revolutionary like those that turned Harley-Davidson's old flathead into the 61 OHV in 1936. Even so, the new model was even more popular than the old, and 12,924 were sold.

The evolution continued in the years that followed. For 1949, hydraulic forks were introduced, giving rise to the first official Harley-Davidson name for the OHV Big Twin: Hydra-Glide. During the early 1950s, the motor was gradually updated, the styling was changed slightly, and a foot-operated shifter and hand-operated clutch was introduced. In 1958, rear suspension was added, giving rise to the second official Harley-Davidson name for the Big Twin: Duo-Glide. In the late 1950s and early 1960s, the British invasion waned, and Harley-Davidson was forced to weather a new invasion, this time by the Japanese. Harley-Davidson stayed on course, however, and their Panhead continued to evolve into a larger, heavier, touring-oriented machine. In 1965, electric starting was added for the Panhead's final year, sparking the third official Harley-Davidson name for the Big Twin: Electra Glide.

In the beginning, the Panhead still was a fairly trim machine that many riders proved was capable of winning on

Coffman's red 1947 Knucklehead has the late-1947 frame with the much-slimmer steering-head casting.

the tracks, on the hills, and in the swamps of America. By the end, it weighed over 700 pounds in stripped form and more than 800 pounds by the time it was outfitted with fiberglass saddlebags, windshield, dual exhaust, and all the chrome bits that were in fashion. In short, it had become the archetypal American touring machine.

For 1966, the Electra Glide was given a new motor featuring yet another redesign of the top end. It, too, was smoother, quieter, more oil tight, cooler running, and more maintenance free than its predecessor, but not much lighter or more powerful. And it, too, was eventually given a nickname: Shovelhead. Over time, many new features were introduced on the Electra Glide, including an alternator, disc brakes, and a real fairing. Then the chopper craze was given official sanction when Harley-Davidson devolved the Electra Glide into a series of more elemental customs that gave variety to the line-up and appealed to new customers.

This cutaway shows the internal workings of the Knucklehead engine. *Copyright Harley-Davidson Michigan, Inc.*

The oldest living Harley rider in Milwaukee? Valentino "Vick" Domowicz, who was over 90 years old when this photo was taken, still kickstarts and rides his 1947 Knucklehead. After the photos were taken, I rode behind him over to the Juneau Avenue plant where he was to meet Willie G. Despite his age, Vick's still a pretty spirited rider.

Except for the cylinders and heads, the 1947 Knucklehead and 1948 Panhead are nearly identical. The Knuckle is owned by Jim "Aard" Conklin and the Pan by ace restorer Elmer Ehnes. Ehnes restored both machines.

In 1984 came the V2 Evolution engine, the first true fulfillment of the promise made in 1936. The new engine was lightweight and as reliable and as maintenance-free as the best of its competitors. When combined with restyled and updated chassis in new models such as the Softail and FLHT, the Evolution engine finally gave Harley-Davidson's Big Twin true mass-market appeal. As a result, by the early 1990s, the once-ailing Milwaukee firm would again achieve the same dominance in the American marketplace that they had enjoyed at the end of 1947.

But after almost 50 years of change, little really had. From Knucklehead, to Panhead, to Shovelhead, and on to Evo, the basics of the 1936 OHV engine that had made it so appealing remained. In fact, maybe we're all really being a bit myopic by encouraging the continued use of such distinctions.

The truth is, the Knucklehead was never really replaced by the Panhead—or by any of the others, for that matter. To Harley-Davidson and to the enthusiasts of the day, there were no Knuckleheads or Panheads, only 61 or 74 OHVs. Later came the official names, such as those already mentioned and a whole slew of later ones such as Super Glide, Low Rider, Tour Glide, Softail—on and on.

In fact, it wasn't until the V2 Evolution engine was introduced in 1984 that Harley-Davidson even gave an official name to any of its OHV Big Twin engines. The switch from Knucklehead to Panhead that today seems to be such a definitive dividing point in Harley-Davidson history was barely noticed by most riders—and it wasn't accompanied by a name.

As a result, somewhere along the way, enthusiasts found it convenient to coin names to distinguish between the variations on the OHV Big Twin motor. And the names are truly useful, in some ways. But let's not let them disguise the fact that what began with the 1936 61 continues today. The 1936 61 has far more similarities to the 1997 FLSTS Heritage Softail Springer than differences. And that is the Knucklehead's greatest legacy.

Index